AUTODESK® REVIT®
ARCHITECTURE 2015

ESSENTIALS

AUTODESK® REVIT® ARCHITECTURE 2015

ESSENTIALS

Ryan Duell

Tobias Hathorn

Tessa Reist Hathorn

AUTODESK®
Official Press

SYBEX®
A Wiley Brand

Senior Acquisitions Editor: Willem Knibbe
Development Editor: Tom Cirtin
Technical Editor: Jon McFarland
Production Editor: Rebecca Anderson
Copy Editor: Linda Recktenwald
Editorial Manager: Pete Gaughan
Vice President and Executive Group Publisher: Richard Swadley
Associate Publisher: Chris Webb
Book Designer: Happenstance Type-O-Rama
Proofreader: Nancy Carrasco
Indexer: Ted Laux
Project Coordinator, Cover: Todd Klemme
Cover Designer: Wiley
Cover Image: ©Ewelina Peszt / ©Aki Yoshida

Dear Reader,

Thank you for choosing *Autodesk Revit Architecture 2015 Essentials*. This book is part of a family of premium-quality Sybex books, all of which are written by outstanding authors who combine practical experience with a gift for teaching.

Sybex was founded in 1976. More than 30 years later, we're still committed to producing consistently exceptional books. With each of our titles, we're working hard to set a new standard for the industry. From the paper we print on, to the authors we work with, our goal is to bring you the best books available.

I hope you see all that reflected in these pages. I'd be very interested to hear your comments and get your feedback on how we're doing. Feel free to let me know what you think about this or any other Sybex book by sending me an email at contactus@wiley.com. If you think you've found a technical error in this book, please visit http://sybex.custhelp.com. Customer feedback is critical to our efforts at Sybex.

Best regards,

CHRIS WEBB
Associate Publisher, Sybex

For Stacey, Lucely, and Nathaniel—can we take a vacation now please?

—Ryan

For Noelle, growing as I write!

—Tobias

For my family—for instilling in me the simple values of hard work and ambition.

—Tessa

About the Authors

 Ryan Duell is a principal quality assurance analyst for Revit at Autodesk. He holds a bachelor's degree in design computing from Boston Architectural College. He started his career with cbt Architects in Boston, Massachusetts, working on a variety of project teams ranging from single-family residential to large commercial projects. Ryan transitioned into the BIM manager role focusing on Autodesk® AutoCAD® Architecture and Autodesk® Revit® Architecture standards, along with contributing assistance to project teams. At Autodesk he spent several years in the product support organization providing Revit support for end users and enterprise accounts. In addition to Autodesk, Ryan teaches Revit at the Boston Architectural College and contributes to the Revit Clinic blog.

 *Tobias Hathorn* is a licensed architect and user experience designer for Autodesk FormIt. He holds a bachelor's degree in architecture from Kansas State University. He started his career at BNIM architects in Kansas City, Missouri, working on a one-million-square-foot IRS paper-processing center in Revit Architecture. After working as a liaison between BNIM and Moshe Safdie and Associates on the Kansas City Performing Arts Center, Tobias moved to Boston to join the Revit product team in Waltham, Massachusetts. Tobias has honed his knowledge and experience with Revit, especially the graphics and rendering features, over the past seven years in the quality assurance and user experience groups. He is currently working on FormIt, a conceptual design tool to aid in the early stages of a BIM workflow. In his free time, he likes to teach Revit Architecture, bicycle, paint, and play Tetris.

 Tessa Reist Hathorn is a licensed architect and a LEED Accredited Professional with nine years of experience in architecture using Revit. After starting her career at BNIM Architects working on historic renovations and the renowned Kauffman Center for the Performing Arts, she eventually moved to Boston, Massachusetts, to work with Moshe Safdie and Associates, working on high-profile international projects, and later Austin Architects in Cambridge, Massachusetts. Tessa currently works as an architect in the Boulder, Colorado, area at Fänas Architecture and consults for local architecture firms.

ACKNOWLEDGMENTS

Thank you to the countless individuals I had the opportunity to work with during my time at cbt Architects; I appreciate all the opportunities I had. A special thanks to Architexts, for the continual reminder as to what a unique environment an architecture firm can be. Next, I need to give a huge thank-you to Autodesk. I appreciate the inside view and access I have to Revit and the amazingly talented and dedicated people I have the opportunity to work with every day. I need to especially thank my supportive wife, Stacey, and children, who have always been there along the way of my often-demanding day and night activities. You give me the motivation to continuously push ahead. Next, Wiley, this book would never have been possible without your talented staff, editing, and support, so thank you. I can't forget to thank Tobias and Tessa for their dedication to the last edition and showing fantastic teamwork again for 2015.

—Ryan

This has been an exciting year of transitions, changes, growth, and development. To that end I'd like to thank the people who helped me along the way: Rebecca Richkus for your three-dimensional mentorship. Steve Crotty and Trey Klein for your toasts, crawls, spikes, and darths. Erik Egbertson for the pre-class conversations and also for your darths. Erik Snell, for your inevitable pokes. Matt Campbell for your gnarly sketches and bright ideas. Tom Vollaro and Matt Jezyk for the right words at the right time. My parents and Tessa's parents for the grand-parenting! Thanks to Wiley, for making this book happen. Thanks to Ryan, for the solid, ahead-of-schedule work. Thanks to Tessa, for *everything still*.

—Tobias

I'd first like to thank my daughter, Noelle, for teaching me the ability to multi-task. I'm convinced being a working mom increases productivity at both work and home. Thank you to my co-writers: to Ryan, for always being one step ahead of the game, and Tobias, a continuous means of strength and support. Thanks also to our technical editor, Jon McFarland, for making us look better than we actually are. And an enormous thanks to our team at Wiley—Tom Cirtin, Pete Gaughan, Rebecca Anderson, and the rest of the editorial staff—for making everything behind the scenes happen.

—Tessa

Contents at a Glance

CONTENTS

CHAPTER 7   Schematic Design   175

CHAPTER 8   Rooms and Color Fill Plans   189

CHAPTER 12   Drawing Sets   271

CHAPTER 13   Workflow and Site Modeling   297

FOREWORD

It is an understatement to say that the AECO industry is going through the most profound transformation since Brunelleschi's Dome of Santa Maria del Fiore, circa 1446.[1] If we were a less risk-adverse group, we would call it a revolution. But alas, we are not. So we simply call it BIM—building information modeling.

BIM is our change initiative. As humans, we are hardwired to fight change; we are born with an instinct to defend ourselves…and our ideas. So change agents (including you, since you've picked up this book!) must think about practicing BIM holistically:

> BIM is 10 percent technology, 90 percent sociology.

As a leadership member of the AGC/AIA BIMForum, I spend a lot of time thinking about the sociology and management science. As one of the Tocci Building Companies' BIM champions since we formalized our implementation in 2006, I apply frameworks like Deming's Cycle for continuous improvement (Plan, Do, Check, Act) and Tuckman's Stages of Group Development (Forming, Storming, Norming).

I don't spend enough time talking about the 10 percent that instigated the 90 percent and continues to fuel our shared change initiative. The technology is so foundational that it is simply assumed. Perhaps I continue to make the same mistake I did when I was first introduced to BIM. I started using Revit Architecture in 2004. The software was intuitive and logical. Being a novice, I thought that both BIM and Revit were the industry standard! But then and now, we still have work to do.

This is why I'm so grateful that Ryan, Tessa, and Tobias have authored *Autodesk Revit Architecture 2015 Essentials*. They are all dear partners in industry transformation. Yes, they are experienced, talented practitioners. But more than that, they are T-shaped[2], thoughtful individuals who balance technology, process, and humans who need to master the picks and clicks.

---

[1]Filippo Brunelleschi is the poster child for the master builders of the Renaissance. He designed and constructed the dome over the Santa Maria del Fiore cathedral in Florence, Italy. The dome is more than a feat of architecture and engineering; it is a feat of integrated process. Brunelleschi oversaw every aspect of the dome, from the scaffolding design to the transport for the stones.

[2]T-shaped people possess deep capabilities in a specific topic or set of topics (typically technical in nature) but also have a wide breadth of sometimes unusual interests that help them relate to the broad picture. The first-known reference is by David Guest, "The hunt is on for the Renaissance Man of computing," *The Independent* (London), September 17, 1991.

Together, they have crafted a guide to Revit 2015 that takes new users from overwhelmed to informed and then project ready. *Autodesk Revit Architecture 2015 Essentials* isn't just for beginners, though. I've been using Revit for a decade, and I'll be diving into the pages that follow to refresh my skills. I've already flagged the section on conceptual massing; I'm not sure why I haven't gotten the hang of which edge to grab!

Whether you're just getting started or interested in polishing your Revit skills, I'm thrilled you're embracing a practice of continuous learning with *Autodesk Revit Architecture 2015 Essentials*. Happy reading, clicking, and transforming!

Laura Handler
@lhandler
www.lauraehandler.com

INTRODUCTION

Welcome to Autodesk Revit Architecture 2015 Essentials, based on the Autodesk® Revit® Architecture 2015 release.

We have shaped the focus and content of this book from our diverse experience as Revit teachers, writers, users, support specialists, designers, and testers. We have tailored the content to what we think is the most valuable combination of topics and generated exercise files that target these topics. Because we teach Revit Architecture to first-time users, we feel the included content is of most value to our students learning the program for the first time. This book should benefit new Revit Architecture users, as well as long-term users who may not use every aspect of the program on a daily basis and could benefit from revisiting exercises as needed.

Revit Architecture 2015 includes a number of valuable new tools. While each tool may not be considered "essential," we have made an effort to mix new tools, tips, and tricks, along with established features into the context of the text and supporting exercises. The book follows real-life workflows and scenarios and is full of practical examples that explain how to leverage the tools within Revit Architecture. We hope you'll agree that we've succeeded.

Who Should Read This Book

This book is written for architects, designers, students, and anyone else who needs their first exposure to Revit Architecture or has had an initial introduction and wants a refresher on the program's core features and functionality. We've designed the book to follow real project workflows and processes to help make the tools easy to follow, and the chapters are full of handy tips to make Revit Architecture easy to leverage. This book can also be used to help prepare for Autodesk's Certified User and Certified Professional exams. For more information on certification, please visit www.autodesk.com/certification.

What You Will Learn

This book is designed to help you grasp the basics of Revit Architecture using real-world examples and techniques you'll use in everyday design and documentation. We'll explain the Revit Architecture interface and help you find the tools you need as well as help you understand how the application is structured. From there we'll show you how to create and modify the primary components in a building design. We'll show you how to take a preliminary model and add layers of intelligence to help analyze and augment your designs. We'll demonstrate how to create robust and accurate documentation and then guide you through the construction process. Whenever possible we will both teach you Revit and put those newfound skills to use in focused exercises.

As you are already aware, BIM is more than just a change in software; it's a change in architectural workflow and culture. To take full advantage of both BIM and Revit Architecture in your office structure, you'll have to make some changes to your practice. We've designed the book around an ideal, integrated workflow to aid in this transition.

What You Will See

For the 2015 version, Autodesk continues the two flavors of Revit: The first is a "one-box" solution that has Revit Architecture, Structure, and MEP inside the same application, referred to as Revit 2015. The second is the Revit Architecture software you may be used to using, referred to as Revit Architecture 2015. There are some small differences between the applications, but the majority of the user interface is the same.

We want you to be aware that we have based the book and the screen captures on Revit 2015. If you notice small differences, we apologize, but it would be very confusing to base the book on both applications noting all the small differences along the way. However, whichever version you have, you'll still be able to follow the lessons and exercises in the chapters of this book with ease.

What You Need

To leverage the full capacity of this book, we highly recommend you have a copy of Revit Architecture installed on a computer strong enough to handle it. To download the trial version of Revit (offered as Revit 2015), go to www.autodesk .com/revitarchitecture, where you'll also find complete system requirements for running Revit Architecture.

From a software standpoint, the exercises in this book are designed to be lightweight and not computationally intensive. This way, you avoid long wait times to open and save files and perform certain tasks. That said, keep in mind that the Autodesk-recommended computer specs for Revit Architecture are far more than what you need to do the exercises in this book but are *exactly* what you need to work on a project using Revit Architecture.

FREE AUTODESK SOFTWARE FOR STUDENTS AND EDUCATORS

The Autodesk Education Community is an online resource with more than five million members that enables educators and students to download—for free (see website for terms and conditions)—the same software used by professionals worldwide. You can also access additional tools and materials to help you design, visualize, and simulate ideas. Connect with other learners to stay current with the latest industry trends and get the most out of your designs. Get started today at www.autodesk.com/joinedu.

What Is Covered in This Book

Revit Architecture is a building information modeling (BIM) application that has emerged as the forerunner in the design industry. Revit Architecture is as much a change in workflow (if you come from a 2D or CAD environment) as it is a change in software. In this book, we'll focus on using real-world workflows and examples to guide you through learning the basics of Revit Architecture 2015—the *essentials*.

Autodesk Revit Architecture 2015 Essentials is organized to provide you with the knowledge needed to gain experience in many different facets of the software. The book is broken down into the following 14 chapters, most of which contain numerous exercise files:

Chapter 1, "Introducing the Autodesk Revit Architecture Interface," introduces you to the user interface and gets you acquainted with the tools and technology—the workflow—behind the software.

Chapter 2, "Walls and Curtain Walls," helps you build on that initial learning by establishing some of the basic building blocks in architecture: walls.

Chapter 3, "Floors, Roofs, and Ceilings," introduces you to the other basic building blocks: floors, roofs, and ceilings. By the end of the first three chapters you will begin to see how easy it is to create the core elements of your building.

Chapter 4, "Stairs, Ramps, and Railings," explains the basics of stairs, ramps, and railings. These core components are versatile and using them can be a bit tricky, so we'll guide you through the process of creating several types of stairs and railings.

Chapter 5, "Adding Families,"   shows you how to add a core element to your project: families. You use families to create most of your content, and Revit Architecture by default comes with a robust supply.

Chapter 6, "Modifying Families,"   shows you how to take these families and modify them or create your own, making the library of your content limitless.

Chapter 7, "Schematic Design,"   introduces you to conceptual design workflows using Autodesk® FormIt software and Autodesk® SketchBook® Pro software to generate design sketches. Then using those sketches you can take the building design and model it in Revit Architecture.

Chapter 8, "Rooms and Color Fill Plans,"   shows you how to add room elements to your spaces, assign information to them, and create colorful diagrams based on space, department, or any other variable you need.

Chapter 9, "Materials, Visualization, Rendering"   introduces you to visualization tools and techniques. You prepare presentation-quality views of your design in elevation, axonometric, and perspective views.

Chapter 10, "Worksharing,"   discusses how to take your Revit Architecture file into a multiperson working environment. Worksharing allows several people within your office or project team to work on the same Revit Architecture file simultaneously.

Chapter 11, "Details and Annotations,"   focuses on adding annotation to explain your designs. You'll learn how to add detail to your model in the form of dimensions, text, keynotes, and tags and how to embellish your 3D model with additional detailing.

Chapter 12, "Drawing Sets,"   shows you how to take all this information and place those drawings and views onto sheets so they can be printed and distributed to your project stakeholders.

Chapter 13, "Workflow and Site Modeling,"   provides the basics on how to take your office from a CAD environment to one that works with BIM. This chapter explores tools for every level of the project team—from the new staff to project managers. Understanding the process and workflow will be key to the success of your first Revit Architecture project.

Chapter 14, "Repeating Objects, Best Practices, and Quick Tips,"   covers different approaches to repeat objects throughout your project along with optimizations, best practices, and tips to use along the way.

The Essentials Series

The Essentials series from Sybex provides outstanding instruction for readers who are just beginning to develop their professional skills. Every Essentials book includes these features:

- ▶ Skill-based instruction with chapters organized around projects rather than abstract concepts or subjects.

- ▶ Digital files (via download) so you can work through the project tutorials yourself. Please check the book's web page at www.sybex .com/go/revit2015essentials for the companion downloads.

  At the book's web page, you'll also find a special bonus file full of suggestions for additional exercises related to each chapter, so you can practice and extend your skills.

 NOTE Should you choose to browse the book's companion web page, it will look like a site to purchase the book, which it is. But if you pan down just a bit, you'll see three gray tabs. The third one is the book's companion downloads.

Contacting the Authors

We welcome your feedback and comments. You can find the three of us on Facebook at Mastering Revit. We hope you enjoy the book.

CHAPTER 1

Introducing the Autodesk Revit Architecture Interface

After more than a decade of use in the architecture, engineering, and construction (AEC) industry, Autodesk® Revit® Architecture software continues to be unique in its holistic building information modeling (BIM) approach to design. There are other tools that allow you to design in 3D, and 10 years ago 3D might have been a differentiator, but today 3D is the standard. BIM is quickly becoming the standard as well.

Revit Architecture provides the unique ability to design, update, and document your project information from within a single file — something no other BIM tool allows you to do. Because all of your data resides in a single project file, you can work in any view to edit your model — plan, section, elevation, 3D, sheets, details, even a schedule — and then watch as your file updates in all views automatically. To begin your journey of learning Revit Architecture, we'll help you become comfortable with the user interface and the basic steps of the Revit Architecture workflow.

In this chapter, you'll learn to:

▶ **Use the Properties palette**

▶ **Use the Project Browser**

▶ **Use the View Control Bar**

▶ **Navigate with the ViewCube**

▶ **Create floors, walls, and levels**

▶ **Change a wall type**

▶ **Place doors and windows**

▶ **Space elements equally**

Understanding the User Interface

The user interface (UI) of Revit Architecture is similar to other Autodesk products such as the Autodesk® AutoCAD®, Autodesk® Inventor, and Autodesk® 3ds Max® products. You might also notice that it's similar to Windows-based applications such as Microsoft Word. All of these applications are based on the "ribbon" concept: Toolbars are placed on tabs in a *ribbon* across the top of the screen. The ribbon is contextually updated based on the elements you have selected. We'll cover the most critical aspects of the UI in this section, but we won't provide an exhaustive review of all toolbars and commands. You'll gain experience with a variety of tools as you read the chapters and go through the exercises in this book.

Figure 1.1 shows the Revit Architecture UI with labels illustrating the major UI elements. Four project views are tiled to display at the same time: plan, elevation, 3D, and perspective camera.

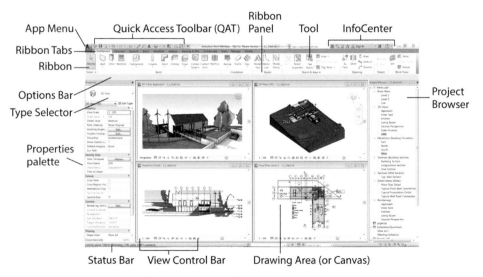

FIGURE 1.1 Revit Architecture user interface

Exercise 1.1: Use the Properties Palette to See Dynamic Updates of Properties

The Properties palette is a floating palette that remains open while you work in the model. The palette dynamically updates to show the properties of the element you have selected. If you have nothing selected, then the view's properties are displayed.

To begin, go to the book's web page at www.sybex.com/go/revit2015essentials, download the files for Chapter 1, and open the file c01-ex-01.1start.rvt. You can open a Revit Architecture project file by dragging it directly into the application or by using the Open command from the Application menu.

1. Go to the Modify tab of the ribbon, find the Properties panel on the far left side of the ribbon, and click the Properties button. This button will open or close the Properties palette. Leave the Properties palette open.

2. Go to the View tab of the ribbon, find the Windows panel to the far right, click the User Interface button, and uncheck or check the Properties option. This will also open or close the Properties palette. Leave the Properties palette open.

3. Move your mouse into the drawing area, or canvas, and then right-click with the mouse; this will bring up a context menu. Click the word *Properties* near the bottom of the list. This will also open or close the Properties palette.

4. You can also toggle the visibility of the Properties palette by pressing Ctrl+1 on your keyboard.

5. The palette can be docked on either side of your screen or left floating in your canvas. To move the palette, just click the Properties palette header and drag it with your mouse. You will see an outline preview of the palette to aid you in placement; release the mouse button to place the palette.

6. To dock the palette back to the left side of the screen, click and drag the mouse *all the way* to the left side of the screen, until the preview outline spans the entire height of the screen. The Properties palette may be up against the Project Browser. You will move the browser to the right side of the screen in the next section. See Figure 1.2.

The Properties palette can be pulled outside the Revit application frame. This is especially helpful if you have a second monitor. You can move the palette to a second screen for maximum Revit canvas space on the primary screen.

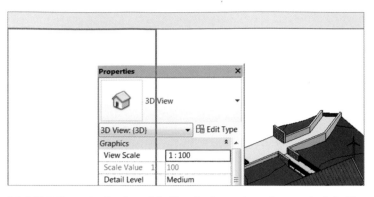

FIGURE 1.2 Preview of docking the Properties palette to the left side

The Properties palette displays Element properties. Changes made in the Properties palette will affect only the currently selected elements. Changes made in the Type Properties dialog (found by clicking the Edit Type button, below the Type Selector) will affect all elements of that particular type, whether they are selected or not.

7. Make sure you don't have any elements selected; look in the Properties palette and notice that it displays the properties of the active view, the 3D view. Use the scroll bar on the right side of the Properties palette to find the Extents group of properties. Check the Crop View option. You don't need to use the Apply button to commit the change; instead just move your mouse into the canvas to automatically apply your changes.

8. Select the red roof in the 3D view. Notice that the Properties palette updates to show the properties of the current selection, the Basic Roof SG Metal Panels Roof. Any changes to these properties will affect this Roof element only.

9. While you still have the roof selected, click the Type Selector dropdown at the top of the Properties palette. Choose the Warm Roof - Timber option from the list. Click your mouse off into space to deselect the roof. You'll notice that the roof is no longer red. When you choose another type from the list, you are swapping the current roof type for another roof with different *type properties*, but the *element properties* stay the same!

This concludes Exercise 1.1. You can compare your results with the sample file c01-ex-01.1end.rvt available in the files you downloaded from the Sybex website.

Exercise 1.2: Explore the Content of Your Project with the Project Browser

The Project Browser (refer back to Figure 1.1) is a table of contents for your project. The structure of the browser is a tree consisting of all the views, legends, schedules, renderings, sheets, families, groups, and links in your Revit Architecture project.

To begin the next exercise, open the file c01-ex-01.2start.rvtfrom the files you downloaded.

1. Much like the Properties palette, the Project Browser can be docked on either side of the Revit canvas. Follow steps 5 and 6 in the previous exercise, but drag the Browser to the right of the canvas as in Figure 1.1.

2. The Project Browser is set up as a tree view with + and – icons to expand or collapse the tree structure. Find the very top node of the Browser named Views (All). Click the - icon found to the left of the Views (All) node.

3. Now click the – icon next to the other top-level nodes: Legends, Schedules/Quantities, Sheets (All), Families, Groups, and Revit Links. Now your Project Browser looks very small, but in reality there are many pieces of content loaded in the current project.

4. Expand the Families node. Find the Planting folder and expand that. Then expand the RPC Tree - Deciduous folder.

5. Find the Hawthorn - 25′ family. Click the text, and drag your mouse onto the canvas. Release the mouse button, and you will see an outline preview to help you place the tree. Click again to place the tree anywhere on the green landscape. The browser allows this nice drag-and-drop workflow for placing content!

6. The Project Browser has a search utility as well. If you right-click any element in the Browser, you will see a Search option at the bottom of the context menu. Click Search, and in the dialog that appears type **Kitchen**; then click the Next button. The search utility opens folders to find any project content with the word *Kitchen* in the title. Find the Rendering: Kitchen view under Sheets (All) ➤ A001 - Title Sheet (Figure 1.3).

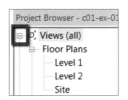
The Project Browser can also be dragged outside the Revit canvas. This comes in very handy if you are using multiple monitors and want to maximize your drawing area.

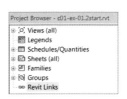

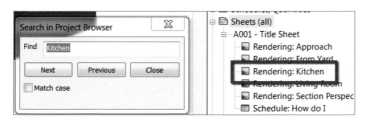

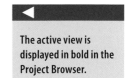
The active view is displayed in bold in the Project Browser.

FIGURE 1.3 Project Browser search results for *Kitchen*

7. Once you've found the Rendering: Kitchen view, close the Search In Project Browser dialog and open the Kitchen view by double-clicking the view name in the Project Browser. A very nice rendering opens; read Chapter 9 to learn how to use Revit's rendering features.

This concludes Exercise 1.2. You can compare your results with the sample file c01-ex-01.2end.rvt in the files you downloaded for this chapter.

By default, the Project Browser displays all of your content; you can filter and customize what you see in the Browser. Right-click Views (All) at the top of the Browser; then select Browser Organization.

Exercise 1.3: Use the View Control Bar to See Frequently Used View Properties

The View Control Bar is at the bottom-left corner of every view. It is a shortcut for frequently used view properties. In most cases you can find the same parameter in the Properties palette for the current view. It is important to note that these commands affect only the currently active view (Figure 1.4).

FIGURE 1.4 The View Control Bar for a 3D view

Open the file c01-ex-01.3start.rvt to begin this exercise.

1. Hover your mouse over the icons on the View Control Bar to see a tooltip, which displays the name of the specific tool. The first icon is Scale, and the second is Detail Level; we won't be changing these view properties in this exercise.

2. The third icon is a cube called Visual Style; click this icon and choose Realistic from the list that pops up. Note that you now see material textures on the walls and site if you zoom in closely. Also, the trees look more realistic.

3. Click the Visual Style icon again; this time click Hidden Line from the list. This is a more traditional black-and-white style for viewing your 3D model.

4. The next icon on the View Control Bar is Sun Path; skip this one. The next icon is Shadows; click this icon and you should see shadows render in your scene.

5. The next icon is a teapot, and it launches the Rendering dialog. The rendering workflow is covered in Chapter 9. Click the teapot icon again to close the Rendering dialog.

6. The next icon is Crop View. This is a very important tool, so click it now. You should see parts of your model around the corners disappear! The model is not deleted, just cropped.

7. The next icon on the View Control Bar is Show Crop Region. Click this to see the crop box for the view. Now that you see it, select it and use the blue grips that appear to adjust your crop as you desire. See Figure 1.5 for an example.

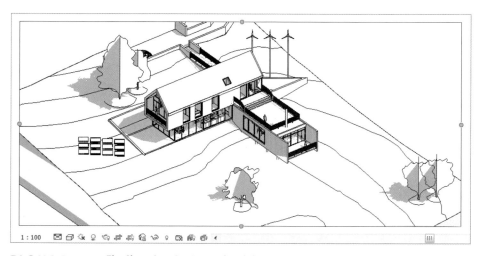

1 : 100

FIGURE 1.5 The Show Crop Region tool and the View Control Bar

The next icon is Lock 3D View. This option is available only in 3D views. The command is helpful if you ever add text to a 3D view and you don't want the viewpoint to change.

8. The next icon looks like sunglasses. The Temporary Hide/Isolate tool is very useful as your project grows more complex. Select the roof in your project, and then click the sunglasses. Choose the option Isolate Element from the dialog. Notice that all other elements in the view are hidden so you can focus on the roof only. Click the sunglasses again, and choose Reset Temporary Hide/Isolate. Now your view is back to normal.

9. The next icon in the View Control Bar is the light bulb, for Reveal Hidden Elements mode. Click the light bulb and a magenta border surrounds your view. Any element that is hidden, or turned off, will also be displayed with magenta lines. This viewing mode will prove

very helpful in locating elements that appear in some views but not your current view. Click the light bulb on the View Control Bar again to return to your normal working mode.

There are other tools on the View Control Bar, but they aren't used frequently enough to be discussed at this time. This concludes Exercise 1.3. You can compare your results with the sample file `c01-ex-01.3end.rvt` in the files you downloaded previously.

Exercise 1.4: Navigate with the ViewCube

As one of several navigation aids in Revit Architecture, the ViewCube is located in the upper-right corner of 3D views. This is a familiar UI element that appears in many Autodesk products.

To begin this exercise, open the file `c01-ex-01.4start.rvt`.

1. Click the face of the ViewCube that is labeled Front. The view dynamically orbits to show a straight-on, elevation-style view of your project — and it will automatically fit the view to the entire model.

2. Move your mouse over the ViewCube. As you hover the mouse, arrows appear on each side of the Front face. Click the arrow to the left of the Front face. The view will dynamically orbit to the Left elevation of your project.

3. Hover your mouse over the ViewCube again; this time click the arrow above the ViewCube. This will take you to a Top view, or plan view orientation, of your project.

4. Hover your mouse over the lower-right corner of the ViewCube top. Click this corner and the view will dynamically orbit back to a 3/4 corner view like you started out in.

5. Now click your mouse anywhere on the ViewCube and drag the mouse. This is a custom orbit, not a predefined angle like Front, Left, or Top. Notice that a green Pivot icon appears at the center of the model. Release the mouse when you like your camera angle. The model does not Zoom To Fit with this type of orbiting.

6. Select one of the trees in the model; then click and drag the ViewCube again. Notice that the green Pivot icon is now in the middle of the selected element. This is a very useful technique for navigating large models if you're editing a specific element.

7. If you are using a mouse, then the scroll wheel is ideal for zooming in and out. If you don't have a mouse, the Zoom controls are all under the magnifying glass near the ViewCube.

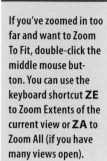

8. Once you've navigated the view and you're satisfied with the camera angle, it is important to save the current viewpoint. Hover your mouse anywhere over the ViewCube and right-click. Select the Save View option from the context menu. Name your view (preferably something specific), and click OK.

9. This will save the angle but not the zoom level. If you want to maintain a certain zoom level, use the View Crop commands covered in steps 6 and 7 of the previous exercise to limit the view to what is most relevant.

If you've zoomed in too far and want to Zoom To Fit, double-click the middle mouse button. You can use the keyboard shortcut ZE to Zoom Extents of the current view or ZA to Zoom All (if you have many views open).

This concludes Exercise 1.4. You can compare your results with the sample file c01-ex-01.4end.rvt.

Creating a Simple Layout

In this section, you'll use the Revit Architecture interface to complete basic modeling workflows. You can apply the basic concepts in these exercises to a variety of tools throughout the program.

Exercise 1.5: Create a Floor

To begin, open the file c01-ex-01.5start.rvt from the files you downloaded at the beginning of this chapter.

1. The project opens in a floor plan view. There are a series of green reference planes for you to use as guides for this exercise. Click the Architecture tab of the ribbon, and find the Floor tool in the Build panel; click the Floor tool to enter Floor sketch mode.

Floor

2. Note that the ribbon adjusts to indicate that you are in a sketch mode. The most obvious indication is the Mode panel with the red X and green check mark icons. These allow you to cancel out of sketch mode or commit your changes. You need to draw your floor shape before you click the green check mark.

Mode

3. The Draw gallery to the right of the Mode panel has many different drawing tools. You'll use the Pick Lines tool since there are reference lines already in place. Click the second-to-last icon in the lower-right corner of the Draw gallery.

Draw

4. Hover your mouse over one of the reference lines, and notice that it highlights to show a preview of the line that will be created. Click each of the reference lines only once. A pink sketch line appears after each click. When you're finished you should see an image similar to Figure 1.6.

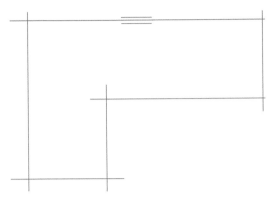

F I G U R E   1 . 6   Floor sketch lines based on reference planes

5. Try clicking the green check mark in the ribbon to commit your sketch lines. You will get an error about intersecting lines. Click Continue, and you will resolve this error. Revit requires that sketches be closed loops, and you have overlapping intersections at each of the corners.

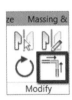

6. Find the Trim/Extend To Corner tool in the Modify panel of the Modify | Create Floor Boundary tab in the ribbon. Click the tool and hover your mouse over a portion of one of the sketch lines that you want to keep; it highlights blue. Then click the line. Next, click the portion of the intersecting line that you wish to keep. Revit will trim the unwanted segments from the corner.

7. After the first corner is cleaned up, Revit remains in the Trim/Extend To Corner tool; click the next two intersecting lines to clean up their corner. Repeat these steps until each corner is cleaned up, as in Figure 1.7.

The status bar in the lower-left corner of the UI provides feedback when using commands like Trim. It also displays keyboard shortcuts as you type, and it reports what object your mouse is hovering over.

8. Finally, click the green check mark; this time you should be successful. Revit has the floor selected when you exit sketch mode. You should see the blue selection color, and you can review your floor's properties in the Properties palette. The floor is on Level 1, and its Area is 2500 SF (762 m).

FIGURE 1.7 Floor sketch lines after trimming the corners

This concludes Exercise 1.5. You can compare your results with the sample file `c01-ex-01.5end.rvt`.

Exercise 1.6: Create Walls

Open the file `c01-ex-01.6start.rvt` to start this exercise.

Wall

1. Find the Wall tool in the Architecture tab of the ribbon. Click the Wall tool and choose the Pick Lines tool from the Draw gallery.

2. Turn your attention to the Properties palette. You will set a few parameters *before* you draw your walls. Change the Location Line parameter by clicking in the cell and choosing Finish Face: Exterior from the drop-down list.

3. Also in the Properties palette, change the Top Constraint parameter to Up To Level: Level 2.

4. Now hover your mouse over one of the edges of the floor. Do not click your mouse yet. Notice the light-blue dotted line that appears. This line indicates whether the wall will be placed inward or outward from the reference line. Note that you may need to zoom in to see the blue dotted line.

5. You want your walls to be inward from the green reference line, so move your mouse slightly inward from the floor edges — until the blue dotted line is on the inside — then click your mouse. Repeat for each edge until your drawing looks similar to Figure 1.8.

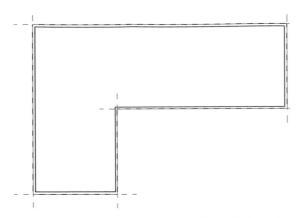

FIGURE 1.8 Walls placed inward from the floor edge

This concludes Exercise 1.6. You can compare your results with the sample file c01-ex-01.6end.rvt.

Exercise 1.7: Create Levels

In Revit Architecture, project datums are very important. Reference planes, grids, and levels are considered datums. These elements are usually visible only in a 2D view. They can be used to move any model element that references them.

To begin, open the file c01-ex-01.7start.rvt.

Remember that you can zoom and pan with the mouse while in the middle of commands like Trim or Offset.

1. In the Project Browser, under the Views (All) node, locate the Elevations (Building Elevation) node, and double-click the North view. You may need to click the + symbol to expand the tree.

2. Zoom in to the right side of the view, and note the graphic representation of Level 1 and Level 2. Select the level line for Level 2, and notice that both the name of the level and the elevation value turn blue.

3. Click the elevation value for Level 2, and change it from 10′-0″ (3000 mm) to 15′-0″ (4500 mm). Zoom out so you can see the walls. Notice that the walls automatically adjust to the new height of Level 2! This happens because the Level datum drives the Top Constraint parameter that was set when the walls were created.

4. Go to the Architecture tab in the ribbon, and find the Datum panel. Click the Level command. Choose the Pick Lines tool from the Draw gallery.

5. Turn your attention to the Options Bar just below the ribbon. Verify that the Make Plan View check box is checked. Then change the Offset value to 15'-0" (4.57 m).

6. Move your mouse into the drawing area and hover over the elevation line of Level 2. Wait until you see the light-blue dotted line appear above Level 2. If you don't see the preview line, then move your mouse slightly up. Click to place your new level.

7. Revit automatically names the new level for you based on the last level created. So in this case, Level 3 is the correct sequence and you don't need to rename it. If you did want to rename the new level, you'd select the level line and click the level name after it turns blue. Press Esc to exit the Level tool.

8. Select Level 3, and click the Copy tool on the Modify tab in the ribbon. Click anywhere in the canvas to specify a start point for the Copy command; then move the mouse in an upward direction. Type 12'-0" (3.657 m), and then press Enter to complete the command. Note that you can press and hold the Shift key to force Copy or Move commands to operate in 6" (100 mm) increments.

9. Select the newest level, and change the name to **Roof**. Note that the level symbol is black, not blue like the others. This means there is not a corresponding plan view for this level.

10. Go to the View tab in the ribbon, find the Create panel, click Plan Views, and then click Floor Plan. The New Floor Plan dialog appears. Only levels that don't have views are listed. In this case, you should see only the Roof level. Click OK to create a new view associated with this level.

You can double-click the blue level markers to open the plan view associated with that level. You can also double-click any blue view symbol such as a section marker, elevation tag, or a callout head.

Switch Windows

11. The new floor plan for the Roof level opens. Go to the View tab of the ribbon, locate the Windows panel, and click Switch Windows. This drop-down list shows all of the views you currently have open. You can click any view to switch to it.

The Switch Windows tool is also located in the Quick Access toolbar (QAT). The keyboard shortcut to cycle through open views is to hold down Ctrl and press the Tab key.

CLOSING UNNEEDED VIEWS

If you have many views open at once, then the performance of Revit Architecture slows down. Be sure to close views when you don't need them anymore. The Close Hidden Windows command in the View tab of the ribbon will close all views but the currently active one. If you have more than one project open, this command leaves open only one view from each project. This tool is most effective if your view windows are full screen.

Close Hidden

This concludes Exercise 1.7. You can compare your results with the sample file c01-ex-01.7end.rvt.

Exercise 1.8: Change Wall Type

In the previous exercise, you created an additional level, thus increasing the overall height of your building. In the following steps, you'll adjust the top constraint of the walls and use the Type Selector to swap generic walls for a more specific wall type.

To begin, open the file c01-ex-01.8start.rvt.

3D View

1. Go to the View tab of the ribbon, find the Create panel, and click the 3D view icon. Also you can click Default 3D View in the QAT, or double-click the {3D} view in the Project Browser.

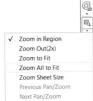

√ Zoom in Region
Zoom Out(2x)
Zoom to Fit
Zoom All to Fit
Zoom Sheet Size
Previous Pan/Zoom
Next Pan/Zoom

2. Click the Close Hidden Windows button in the QAT, and then activate the South view under Elevations (Building Elevation) from the Project Browser.

3. From the View tab in the ribbon, locate the Windows panel, and then click the Tile Windows button. You can also use the keyboard shortcut **WT**. You should see the two active views (default 3D view and South elevation) side by side.

4. In either view, find the Navigation bar, click the drop-down arrow under the Zoom icon, and then click Zoom All To Fit. You can also use the keyboard shortcut **ZA**.

5. Find the Modify button at the far left side of the ribbon. Click the Select button under the Modify button and a drop-down appears. Make sure that the Select Elements By Face option is checked. This will enable easier selection of walls.

6. Click inside the 3D view window to activate the view. Hover the mouse pointer over any of the walls. Press the Tab key once, and all of the walls should highlight, as in Figure 1.9. The status bar should indicate "Chain of walls or lines." Click the mouse once to select the chain of walls.

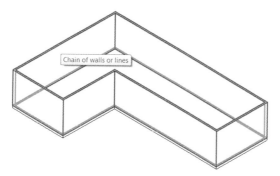

FIGURE 1.9 Highlighted walls of a chain selection

7. With the walls still selected, turn your attention to the Properties palette. Find the parameter Top Constraint. Change the value to Up To Level: Roof, and then click Apply, or move your mouse into the canvas to automatically apply it. Notice how the walls change height in both the 3D view and the elevation view (Figure 1.10).

Use the chain-select method on anything from walls to lines in sketches to detail lines.

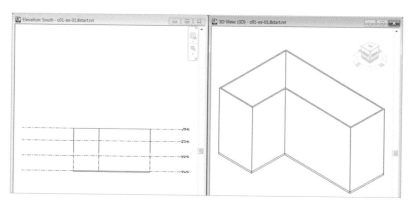

FIGURE 1.10 Tiled windows show the result of modifying the top constraints of the walls.

Changing wall segments from one wall type to another is similar to changing a font in Microsoft Word. You select the sentence and then choose a different font from the font selector — the words stay the same, but the style changes.

8. Review Figure 1.1 to see the intended image. In the 3D view, select the wall that corresponds to the Front face of the ViewCube. Press and hold the Ctrl key, and select the wall segments adjacent to it, as in Figure 1.11.

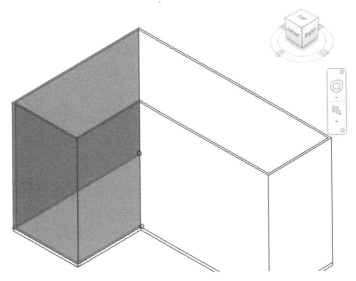

FIGURE 1.11 Use the Ctrl key to manually select multiple items in your model.

9. With the walls selected, look to the top of the Properties palette to find the Type Selector. Note that it is reporting that the wall type of the current selection set is Basic Wall Generic - 8″ (200 mm). Click the Type Selector to open a list of wall types in the project. Choose the Exterior - Brick On CMU wall type near the top of the list.

10. Zoom into the walls for which you just swapped types. The thickness of these three walls should update to inherit the properties of the type you chose. Also, if you zoom in close enough, you should see a brick pattern on the walls, which the Generic walls did not have.

This concludes Exercise 1.8. You can compare your results with the sample file c01-ex-01.8end.rvt.

Exercise 1.9: Place Interior Walls

Open the file c01-ex-01.9start.rvt to begin this exercise.

1. From the Architecture tab in the ribbon, click the Wall tool. Use the Type Selector to change the wall type — *before placing the walls* — to Interior – 4 7/8″ (123 mm) Partition (1-hr).

2. In the Draw gallery in the ribbon, choose the Pick Lines icon; then click each of the green reference planes that have been provided as guides for interior walls. Your results should resemble Figure 1.12.

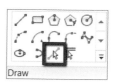

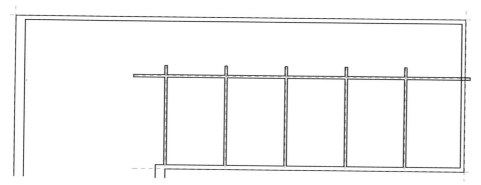

FIGURE 1.12 The interior walls

3. Choose the Trim/Extend Multiple Elements tool from the Modify tab of the ribbon. Select the long horizontal interior wall first. Then move your mouse inside the room on the lower-right side of the plan. Hold your mouse button down and drag a crossing selection window up and to the left to include each of the smaller segments of wall. Release the mouse, and Revit should trim off the walls neatly, as in Figure 1.13.

The Function parameter of a wall helps define its default height options. For example, an interior wall defaults to the level shown in step 1, whereas an exterior wall is set to Unconnected Height.

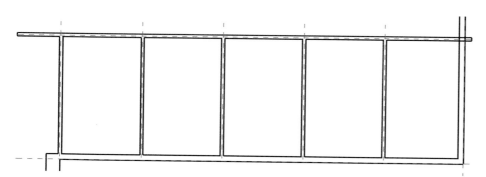

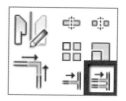

FIGURE 1.13 Results of Trim/Extend Multiple Elements

4. Select the Trim/Extend Single Element tool from the Modify tab of the ribbon. First, click the exterior wall to the far right of the plan. Then click the intersecting interior wall. Remember, Revit's Trim tool wants you to click the segments you want to keep.

5. Now select the Trim/Extend To Corner tool from the Modify tab. Click the remaining overlapping corners to clean up the wall construction.

6. Note that the leftmost interior wall is not aligned with the thicker Brick On CMU wall. Click the Align tool from the Modify tab of the ribbon. First, click the inside edge of the thicker wall because that is what you want to align to. The second click should be on the outside edge of the leftmost interior wall. This is what you want to move. The results should resemble Figure 1.14.

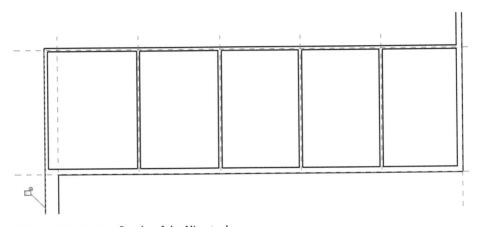

FIGURE 1.14   Results of the Align tool

This concludes Exercise 1.9. You can compare your results with the sample file c01-ex-01.9end.rvt.

Exercise 1.10: Place Doors and Windows

In this exercise, you'll place doors and windows in the walls. Doors and windows require a wall to host them. You'll use the generic Door and Window families that are loaded in the project, but bear in mind that families of any size, material, and configuration can be used in Revit.

To begin, open the file c01-ex-01.10start.rvt.

1. Go to the Architecture tab and locate the Door tool. Click the tool and notice that the Type Selector reports that the Door type is Single-Flush 36″ (914 mm) × 84″ 2133 mm).

Door

2. Hover the mouse over one of the interior walls, and you'll see a preview of the door being placed in the wall. Press the spacebar and notice that the door flips the direction in which it is swinging.

3. Move the mouse more toward the inside of the room, and press the spacebar until your door swings into the room and is swinging in the correct direction. Click to place the door.

4. Repeat the same steps to place doors into the other rooms along the interior wall. When you finish, the results should appear similar to Figure 1.15.

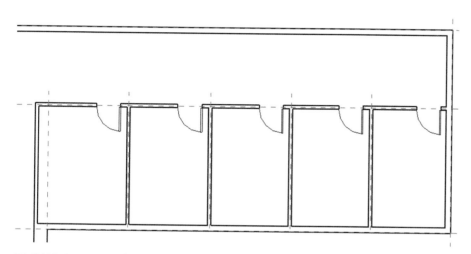

FIGURE 1.15 The doors swing into the rooms.

5. Go back to the Architecture tab of the ribbon and locate the Window tool. Click the tool and notice that the Type Selector reports that the Window type is Fixed 36″ (914 mm) × 48″ (1219 mm).

Window

6. Hover the mouse over one of the exterior walls between the interior walls, and you'll see a preview of the window being placed in the wall. Move the mouse inside the wall to make the window pane closer to the inside of the room as well. Click to place the window.

7. Repeat the same steps to place windows along the exterior wall for each of the interior rooms. When you finish, the results should appear similar to Figure 1.16.

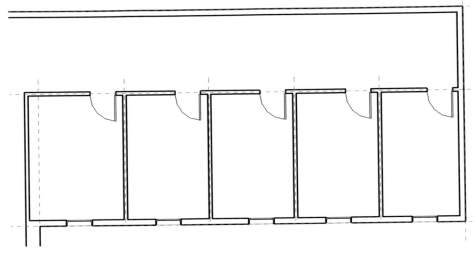

FIGURE 1.16 The Windows for the rooms

> If you happen to place a door or window and you want to change the door swing or the glass placement, just select the element and press the spacebar. Revit will flip the orientation of the family.

This concludes Exercise 1.10. You can compare your results with the sample file c01-ex-01.10end.rvt.

Exercise 1.11: Space Elements Equally

In this exercise, you'll use dimensions and temporary dimensions to create an equally spaced relationship between the interior walls, then the doors, and then the windows. This will illustrate the idea of using constraints to create design intent. This is a fundamental concept of Revit's parametric modeling.

Open the file c01-ex-01.11start.rvt to begin this exercise.

Aligned

1. From the Annotate tab in the ribbon, locate the Dimension panel, and click the Aligned Dimension tool. In the Options Bar, notice that the Placement drop-down is set for Wall Centerlines. Click in this drop-down and change the placement to Wall Faces.

2. Hover your mouse over the leftmost interior wall, and you should see the outside edge highlight. Click to start a dimension string.

3. Return your attention to the Options Bar and change the placement from Wall Faces to Wall Centerlines.

4. Move your mouse back into the canvas and hover over the center of the interior walls until you see a blue highlight in the center of the interior walls. Click to continue your dimension string. Repeat for each interior wall.

5. Return to the Options Bar and change the placement from Wall Centerlines to Wall Faces. Click the inside face of the exterior wall to finish adding dimensions to your dimension string.

6. Move your mouse above the interior wall and click to place the dimension string in the view. The results should resemble Figure 1.17.

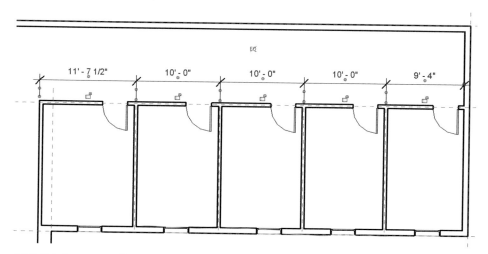

FIGURE 1.17 The dimensions of the interior walls

7. After placing the dimension string, notice the blue EQ icon that appears. This is a valuable shortcut for spacing your elements evenly. Click this icon and your walls will automatically space themselves evenly.

8. You will most likely get an error because of a door overlapping with a wall. Disregard this warning by closing the small dialog that opens in the lower-right corner. We will use temporary dimensions to help space the doors in the next step. Click the Esc key twice to exit the Dimension tool.

9. Select the rightmost door, and notice the light-blue dimensions that appear. These are called temp dims and are very helpful for locating doors and windows relative to walls. Notice that this door is 2'-6" (.76m) from the wall. This is perfect; leave it as is.

If you want to see the actual dimension values instead of EQ in your dimension strings, right-click the dimension string and select EQ Display to toggle between the two settings. You should see the EQ icon display anytime you select a dimension string.

10. Select the next door to the left and hover your mouse over the temp dim that appears. The tooltip lets you know you can edit this dimension. Click the blue text and type 2'-6" (.76m) into the text box. The door moves to the correct location. Follow these steps for the other doors. The results should resemble Figure 1.18.

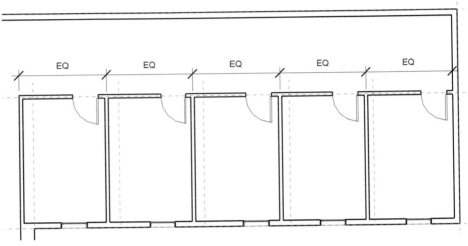

FIGURE 1.18 Doors equally spaced relative to the walls

11. Now you will combine the techniques of using dimensions and temp dims to space the windows equally. Select the rightmost window.

12. The temp dim reference line spans from the center of the window to the center of the exterior wall — turn your attention to the blue circle icon at the center of the exterior wall. Click the blue circle icon once, and the circle jumps to the inside face of the wall. Click the same circle again, and the temp dim appears along the outside face of the exterior wall.

13. Click the temp dim value and change it to 4'-8" (1.42 m).

14. Follow the same steps to make the center of the leftmost window 4'-8"(1.42 m) from the exterior face of the exterior wall.

15. Click the Annotate tab of the ribbon, and choose the Aligned Dimension tool.

16. Hover your mouse over the middle of the leftmost window. You should see a small vertical blue highlight appear, indicating the center of the window. Click to place a dimension reference there.

17. Hover over the middle of the next window and click to continue your dimension string. Repeat until you have a dimension string between the centers of each of the windows.

18. Move your mouse down below the wall, and click to place the dimension string in the view. Click the EQ button that appears. Press Esc to exit the Dimension tool. Your result should resemble Figure 1.19.

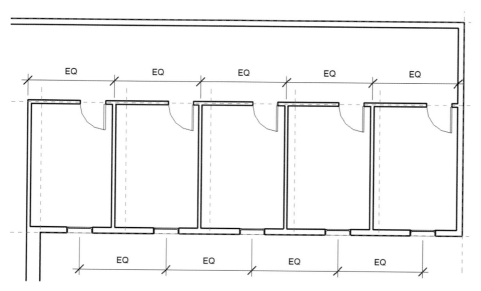

FIGURE 1.19 Windows equally spaced

This concludes Exercise 1.11. You can compare your results with the sample file c01-ex-01.11end.rvt.

Now You Know

The Revit Architecture interface is organized in a logical manner that enforces repetition and therefore increases predictability. Almost every command can be executed by selecting a view from the Project Browser, choosing a tool from the ribbon, specifying settings in the Properties palette, and then placing an element in the drawing window. From there you'll use the View Control Bar and the ViewCube to view your elements as you'd like. Although we covered only the most basic tools like Trim, Align, temp dims, and Aligned Dimensions in the preceding exercises, you'll be able to apply what you've learned in this chapter to the many exercises exploring other tools in subsequent chapters.

CHAPTER 2

Walls and Curtain Walls

Walls in the Autodesk® Revit® Architecture software can range a great deal in complexity. Early in the design process, walls and curtain walls can be more generic, essentially serving as vertical containers for space and function. They can also be associated to masses in order to create incredibly complex shapes. As the design progresses, these generic walls and curtain walls can be swapped out for more specific vertical compound walls that indicate a range of materials as well as geometric sweeps and reveals.

In this chapter, you'll learn to:

▶ **Create walls using several different methods**

▶ **Host elements in walls**

▶ **Modify wall parameters**

▶ **Modify and reset wall profiles**

▶ **Create and customize a curtain wall**

▶ **Embed a curtain wall in a basic wall**

▶ **Add/remove grids and add a curtain wall door**

Understanding Wall Types and Parameters

Revit Architecture has three fundamental types of walls: basic, stacked, and curtain walls. In this section, we will cover some of the important aspects of each. This is not intended to be an exhaustive guide to creating and editing each wall type but rather an overview to provide some background knowledge before we continue with the exercises throughout this chapter.

Basic Walls

The Revit Architecture default template includes several wall types. The most basic wall types have no detailed structure and are named with the prefix Generic for easy identification. Other wall types have highly detailed structures known as layers. Each layer is assigned a function, material, and thickness. The function of a wall layer determines how it will join when multiple wall types intersect or when a wall intersects another element such as a floor.

1. On the Architecture tab in the ribbon, click the Wall tool.

2. In the Type Selector at the top of the Properties palette, select the Generic - 8″ (200 mm) Masonry wall type.

3. Click Edit Type just below the Type Selector.

4. Click the Preview button at the lower left in the Type Properties dialog to see a graphic sample of the wall type.

In Figure 2.1, the structural region of this wall is defined by a diagonal cross-hatch pattern. This is a basic wall with only one pattern defining the wall's material.

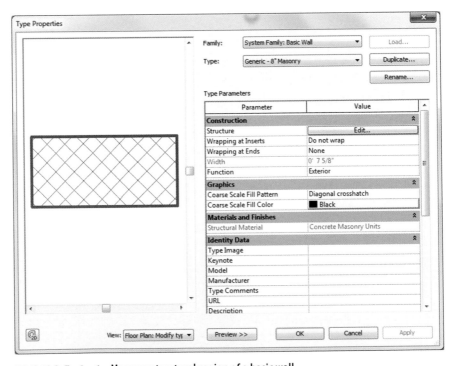

FIGURE 2.1 Masonry structural region of a basic wall

Basic walls can be modified to contain far more structural detail:

1. With the Type Properties dialog still open, go to the Type drop-down.

2. Select the wall type Exterior - Brick On Mtl. Stud, and you'll see the difference (Figure 2.2).

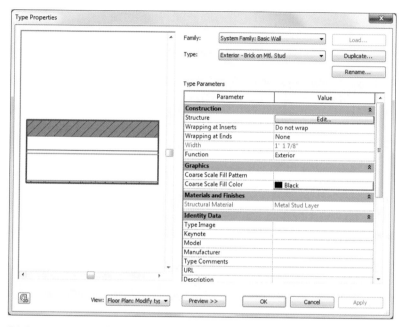

FIGURE 2.2 Compound walls consist of several layers of functional materials.

3. Click the Edit button in the Structure parameter.

Basic walls can even have profiles applied to them that are used to add or remove geometry in your walls. If you're still examining the structure of the previous wall, do the following:

1. Click the Cancel button, and select the wall type Exterior - Brick And CMU On MTL. Stud.

2. In the Preview pane, switch the View to Section.

3. Zoom into the top of the wall sample shown in the preview.

   You'll see a parapet cap at the top of the wall (Figure 2.3). This is a profile associated to the basic wall type.

Notice the numerous values that control the function, material, and thickness for this wall type. These values help you coordinate your project informa-tion across views and schedules.

Although you can manually add profiles to walls in your project on a case-by-case basis, we think you'll find that adding them to the wall definition makes creating and updating wall types easy and quick.

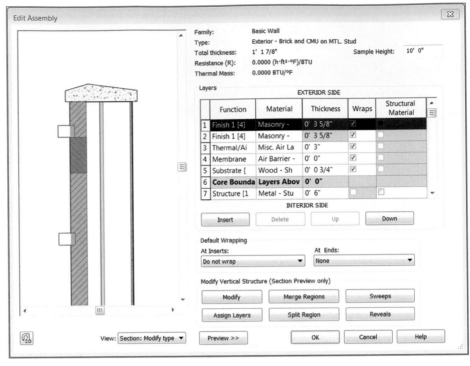

FIGURE 2.3 Wall sweep as part of a wall

Stacked Walls

Stacked walls consist of basic wall types but are combined vertically in a single defined type. Any basic walls can be used to create a stacked wall.

To find the stacked wall types, follow these steps:

1. Start the Wall tool, access the Type Selector, and scroll to the bottom of the list.

2. Select the wall type Exterior - Brick Over CMU w Metal Stud.

3. Click the Edit Type button, and then click Structure Edit.

As shown in Figure 2.4, this wall type is defined by two different basic walls, but you can add more if necessary.

One of the stacked wall segments must be of variable height to accommodate the vertical constraints of the wall instances you place in a project. If all the segments were a fixed height, it would conflict with varying datum geometry in your project. In addition to specifying the height of the segments, you can also adjust the horizontal offset or set a segment to flip its orientation (inside or outside).

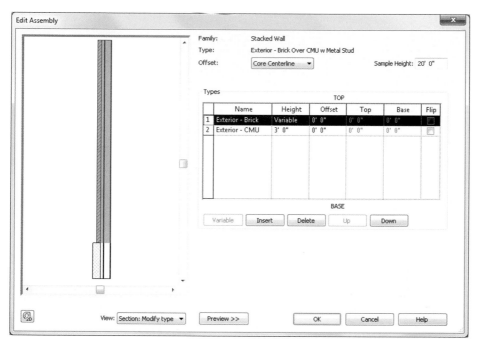

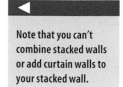

Note that you can't combine stacked walls or add curtain walls to your stacked wall.

FIGURE 2.4 Type properties of a stacked wall

Stacked walls have a unique option available (select and then right-click) called Break Up. When a stacked wall is broken up, the segments are reduced to individual basic walls. The basic walls represent the same dimensions specified in the stacked wall.

Keep in mind there is no method to convert the basic wall segments to the original stacked wall.

Curtain Wall Types

Curtain walls are more complex than basic walls or stacked walls. They consist of four elements: a simple wall-segment definition, curtain grids, panels, and mullions. Curtain wall types can be completely instance based (allowing each to vary) or can be driven entirely by the wall type properties that set grid spacing, panels, and mullion types for interior and border conditions (Figure 2.5).

Hosting Elements in Walls

Walls can host other types of elements that are meant to create openings. As long as the walls exist, the elements they are hosting exist as well. Doors and windows are examples of commonly used hosted elements.

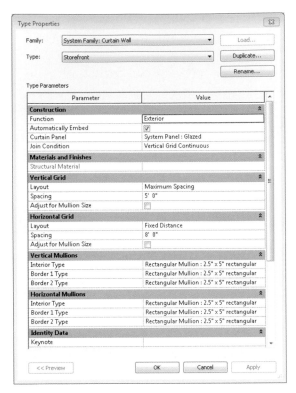

FIGURE 2.5 Curtain wall type definitions

Placing a door in a wall is very easy and can be done in plan, elevation, or 3D view. You may notice that you can place doors only in walls. This is because door families are hosted elements and cannot exist without a host. Because of this relationship, hosted elements are automatically deleted if you delete a host element such as a wall.

Creating Wall Configurations

The objective of the following exercise is to create several different wall configurations through drawing and picking existing geometry. The first method you will explore is manually drawing walls using some of the Draw shapes (Figure 2.6).

FIGURE 2.6 Generic configurations for walls

Then you will use additional wall tools to create arc shapes using Tangent End Arc and Fillet Arc configurations to append wall segments to existing wall elements.

Once the exterior walls are created, the last portion of the exercise will focus on creating walls by picking existing geometry to create walls.

Exercise 2.1: Create Wall Configurations

To begin, go to the book's web page at www.sybex.com/go/ revit2015essentials, download the files for Chapter 2, and open the file c02-ex-2.1start.rvt.

1. Activate the floor plan named Drawing Walls. Start the Wall tool, and practice creating segments of walls using various tools in the Draw panel (such as Line or Center-Ends Arc). Don't worry about where you create these walls; it's just practice. Also take note of the settings available in the Options Bar prior to wall placement because they will vary for each tool.

2. Activate the floor plan named Tangent-Fillet Walls. Your goal is to complete the layout of the walls according to the dashed lines shown in the floor plan.

3. In the upper-right corner of the layout, the two perpendicular walls must be joined with a radius wall segment. Select either one of the wall segments, right-click, and select Create Similar from the context menu.

4. On the Draw panel in the ribbon, select the Fillet Arc option. Click one wall segment and then the other perpendicular segment. After you click the second wall segment, a curved segment appears.

5. Place the curved segment near the layout line. Before you continue, click the radial temporary dimension value and change it to 6′ (2000 mm).

6. The Wall command should still be active, so select the two perpendicular walls in the lower-right corner of the layout, and repeat steps 4 and 5.

7. With the Wall command remaining active, return to the Draw panel in the ribbon, and select the Tangent End Arc option. Click the left end of the wall segment at the bottom of the layout, and then click the left end of the wall segment at the top to complete the tangent arc wall. Your results should look like the plan shown in Figure 2.7.

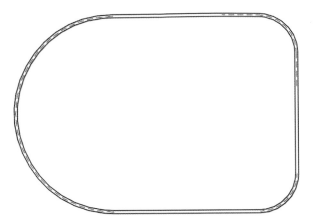

FIGURE 2.7 Results of the Tangent-Fillet Walls steps

8. Activate the Picking Walls floor plan, and then start the Wall tool. Choose the Pick Lines option in the Draw panel in the ribbon. On the Options Bar, set the Location Line to position the wall in relation to the picked path.

9. In the first set of lines in the sample file, pick each individual line segment to place walls.

10. On the second set of lines, use the chain-select method to place all the wall segments at once. Hover your mouse pointer over one of the line segments, and press the Tab key once. When the chain of lines is highlighted, click the mouse button to place the complete chain of walls. Your results should look like the plan shown in Figure 2.8.

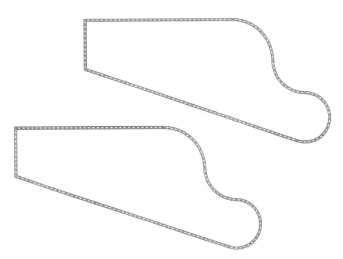

FIGURE 2.8 Result of Pick Lines

CREATING ELLIPTICAL WALLS

Because the need for elliptical walls may occur in your designs, we'll address them now. You should know two things. First, elliptical walls can't be sketched using the Draw tools. Second (and more important), they can be created via workarounds (such as creating an elliptical mass and then picking the face of the mass from which to create an elliptical wall).

So, what's a better way? Create elliptical wall layouts from a series of tangent arcs. Doing so will give you an approximation that is indistinguishable from an actual ellipse, and you'll be able to guide the walls' construction more accurately in the field.

Exercise 2.2: Host a Door in a Wall

To begin, go to the book's web page at www.sybex.com/go/revit2015essentials, download the files for Chapter 2, and open the file c02-ex-2.2start.rvt.

1. Activate the floor plan named Existing Walls.

2. Start the Door tool, and add three doors to the main horizontal wall to the left of the vertical walls.

3. After placing a door, select the door and notice the temporary dimensions that appear.

4. With the door still selected, adjust the temporary dimension so they are 9″ off the center of the perpendicular walls (left-click the temporary dimension Move Witness Line) to toggle the dimension witness line.

5. Click the temporary dimension text, which allows you to enter 9″ (230 mm) (Figure 2.9).

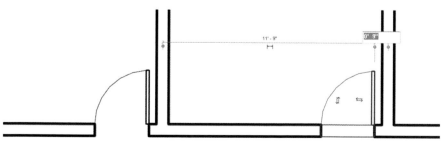

FIGURE 2.9 Hosting doors in a wall

Modifying Wall Parameters

▶

Remember that you can disable the Tag On Placement setting in the Modify | Place Door contextual tab in the ribbon if you wish to toggle whether a tag is also created.

Now that you've created a few wall configurations, it's important to understand how you can modify them. Sometimes this is done simply by selecting the wall and dragging a wall end or a shape handle to a new position. In other cases, you want to be more exact and assign a specific value.

Your approach depends on where you are in the design process. Just remember that you can update design decisions, and all your views, schedules, tagging, and so forth will update—don't get concerned with being too exact early in your design.

The objective of the following exercise is to modify existing wall type and instance parameters. You will start by modifying some type parameters of the wall. Then for the second part you will modify some instance parameters.

Exercise 2.3: Modify Wall Parameters

To begin, go to the book's web page at www.sybex.com/go/revit2015essentials, download the files for Chapter 2, and open the file c02-ex-2.3start.rvt.

1. Activate the floor plan named Level 1. Sketch a straight segment of a wall, but this time as you draw the wall, type **40** (or **12000** mm). Depending on the default units, typing 40 creates a 40′ segment.

   Notice that you didn't have to indicate the units as feet. If you wanted to indicate inches, you'd only have to put a space between the first and second values. Thus, 40′-6″ can easily be entered as 40(space)**6**.

2. Press the Esc key twice, or click the Modify button in the ribbon. Select the segment of wall you just created.

3. There are two options to modify the length, as shown in Figure 2.10. You can type in a new value by selecting the temporary dimension and entering the value, or you can simply drag either wall end to a new location.

FIGURE 2.10 Modifying the wall length

4. Open to the default 3D view by navigating to the View tab and clicking 3D View, and look at some other options. The two blue arrows at

the top and bottom of the wall are called *shape handles* (Figure 2.11). You can click and drag them to adjust the top and bottom locations of a wall. As you drag the shape handle you will see a temporary location line until you release the shape handle.

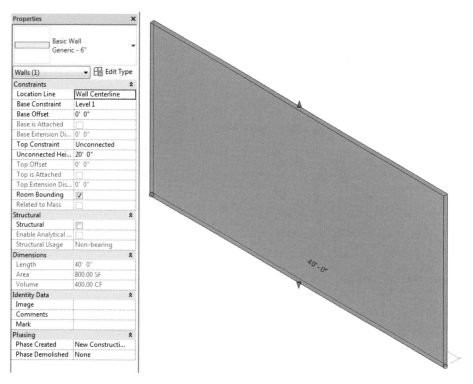

FIGURE 2.11 Shape handles and instance parameters displayed in the Properties palette

5. Next, let's look at the instance parameters. Changes to these parameters will update only the selected instance(s). First, select the wall and review the Properties palette. These are the specific instance parameters for this wall type.

6. Update the Location Line parameter value to be Finish Face: Exterior. The location line is the origin of the wall. If you swap one wall for another, the location line will be maintained. In other words, if you create an exterior wall and the location line is the inside face, then when you change the properties or select a thicker wall, it will grow to the outside—away from the location line.

7. Next, locate the Base Constraint parameter. Change the value to Level 2. The base constraint is the bottom of the wall. The base constraint can be changed at any time, and the wall will move to reflect the change.

8. Locate the Base Offset parameter. Change the value to 1'-0" (300 mm). The Base Offset or Top Offset is the value above or below the respective constraint (negative dimensions can also be used). For example, if you wanted the bottom of a wall associated to Level 1 but 3'-0" (1 m) below, the value for Base Offset would be -3'-0".

9. Locate the Unconnected Height parameter. Change the value to 12'-0" (3655 mm). The Unconnected Height value is the height of the wall when you do not use a specific datum for Top Constraint. If you change the Base Constraint parameter back to Level 1 and then change the Top Constraint value to Up To Level: Level 2, the Unconnected Height parameter becomes inactive.

Editing and Resetting Wall Profiles

Not all walls are rectilinear in elevation, and for these situations you can edit the profile of a wall. Note that you'll be able to edit the profile of a straight wall only, not a curved wall.

When you edit a wall's profile, the wall is temporarily converted to an outline sketch in elevation. Because the sketch is not plan based, you can edit a profile only in a section, an elevation, or an orthogonal 3D view. You can draw as many closed-loop sketches as you like within the wall's profile, but each loop must be closed.

If you need to remove the edited condition of a wall, don't reenter Edit Profile mode and manually remove the sketches. Select the wall, and click Reset Profile in the Mode panel on the Modify | Walls tab. Doing so will reset the extents of the wall and remove any interior sketches.

Another scenario for using Reset Profile would be when attempting to use Attach Top/Base. Depending on how the wall profile was originally edited, Revit could display a join error when attempting to attach the wall. This is most likely to occur if the top of the wall profile was edited previously. Reset the profile first, and then attempt to attach the wall to the roof as needed.

The objective of the following exercise is to edit the profile of a wall from a rectangle to a custom shape and reset the profile at the end of the exercise. Then you will continue with a second exercise using the Attach Top/Base tool to attach one wall to another wall. The last portion of this exercise will cover detaching the condition.

Exercise 2.4: Edit and Reset the Wall Profile

To begin, go to the book's web page at www.sybex.com/go/ revit2015essentials, download the files for Chapter 2, and open the file c02-ex-2.4start.rvt.

1. The starting file should open to the default 3D view. Select the 40′ (12000 mm) wall, and click Edit Profile on the Modify | Walls tab.

2. From the South Elevation view, create the sketch as shown in the top illustration in Figure 2.12.
    Don't worry about following the exact dimensions in this illustration—we're just showing them for reference.

3. Delete the top line, and trim the two side sketch lines.
    Note that the reference lines indicating the extents of the original wall remain, as shown in the bottom illustration in Figure 2.12.

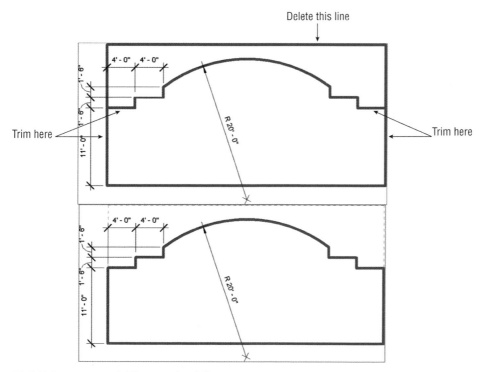

FIGURE 2.12 Adding new sketch lines

4. Use the Trim tools as necessary to clean up the sketch so that it remains as one closed loop.

   If you have crossing lines or open segments, you will receive an error when you attempt to finish the sketch in the next step.

5. When you have finished, click Finish Edit Mode.

Should the design change later and you need to remove the custom wall profile, you can select the wall and use the Reset Profile tool on the ribbon.

Exercise 2.5: Attach and Detach the Top/Base

To begin, go to the book's web page at www.sybex.com/go/revit2015essentials, download the files for Chapter 2, and open the file c02-ex-2.5start.rvt.

1. The starting file should open to the default 3D view. Select the wall and click Edit Profile. Modify the profile sketch as shown in Figure 2.13. Don't forget to trim and delete unnecessary sketch lines. Then finish the sketch.

> You can also use Windows clipboard commands to copy elements. Just remember to paste them to the new location.

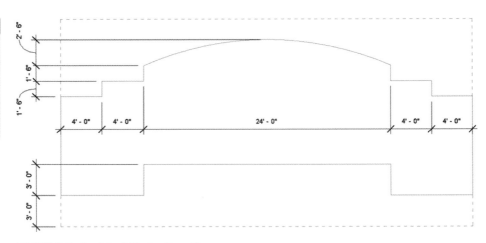

FIGURE 2.13   Edited wall profile

2. Open the Level 1 floor plan, and sketch another wall right on top of the same location as the wall you just edited. In this case, use a Generic 12″ Masonry (305 mm) wall, and set the Unconnected Height in the Options Bar to 2′-0″ (610 mm).

3. Open the default 3D view to complete this step. Select the thicker wall, click Attach Top/Base (Figure 2.14), and confirm that the

Options Bar setting is correct for Top or Base. Now select the wall with the profile that you just edited. This attaches the top of the thicker wall to the underside of the upper wall, as shown on the right side of the figure.

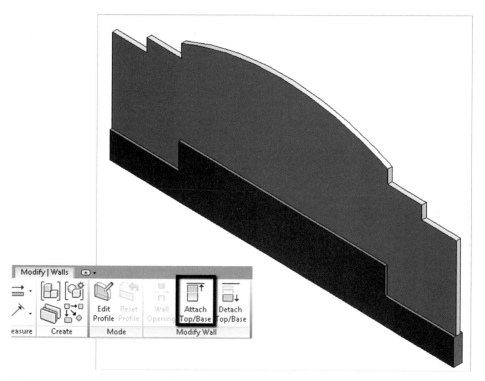

FIGURE 2.14 Attach Top/Base setting

The great thing about this technique is that the relationships between the two walls are maintained if you edit the elevation profile of the upper wall. Performing these steps is a lot faster than having to edit the elevation profile of both walls! If you should need to detach the lower wall, follow the remaining steps in this exercise.

4. Select Generic 12″ Masonry and click Detach Top/Base on the ribbon.

5. Click the Generic 8″ wall above, or click Detach All on the ribbon to reset the wall back to the original 2′-0″ unconnected height.

Cutting Openings

A common use of this technique is to attach walls to sloped elements, such as the underside of roofs.

Openings can be cut in both straight and curved walls. The Wall Opening command tends to be used in curved walls because you already have the option to edit the elevation profile in straight walls. And when you cut an opening, you cannot sketch beyond the extents of the wall boundary or create shapes that are not rectilinear.

The objective of the following exercise is to add and modify wall openings in a curved wall.

Exercise 2.6: Cut Openings in a Curved Wall

To begin, go to the book's web page at www.sybex.com/go/revit2015essentials, download the files for Chapter 2, and open the file c02-ex-2.6start.rvt.

1. The starting file should open to the default 3D view. Select the curved wall.

   The Wall Opening option appears on the Modify | Wall tab, as shown in Figure 2.15 on the left.

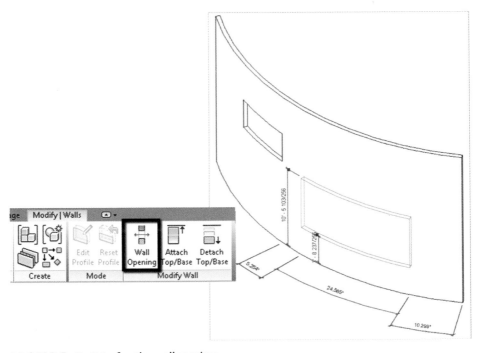

FIGURE 2.15 Creating wall openings

2. Select this command, and then hover over the wall.

You are prompted to create a rectilinear opening with two clicks, as shown in Figure 2.15 on the right.

3. Create two wall openings anywhere in the arc wall.

When the wall opening is selected, the Properties palette will display constraints such as Top Offset and Base Offset. This allows input for exact dimensions to modify the opening size and location.

4. Set the Base Offset to 1'-0" for one of the wall openings.

5. If you need to delete an opening, hover over the opening edge and select it (or use the Tab key to toggle the selection) and then press the Delete key.

Splitting Walls

Sometimes, after you've created walls, you realize that you don't need an inner segment—or you need to change a segment to another wall type. The process of deleting and re-creating walls would be tedious work. However, Revit Architecture offers a Split Element tool on the Modify tab of the ribbon that allows you to divide walls, effectively breaking them into smaller pieces. This can be done along both horizontal and vertical edges of either curved or straight walls (Figure 2.16).

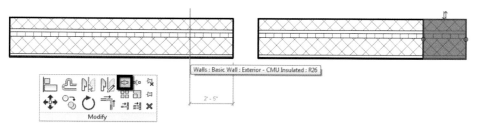

FIGURE 2.16 Splitting walls, before and after

Swapping Walls

Swapping walls for different types prevents the rework of deleting them and creating new ones. Doing so is as easy as selecting a wall and then selecting the new type from the Properties palette (Figure 2.17). This is especially useful early in the design process, when the exact wall type is likely to be unknown. Generic or placeholder wall types can be used and then swapped later on when the design progresses.

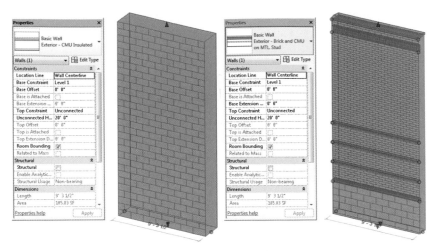

FIGURE 2.17 Swapping wall type before and after

Creating Curtain Walls

Curtain walls are created in much the same way as regular walls: by selecting the type of curtain wall and then sketching the desired shape. However, the available parameters for curtain walls vary from basic or stacked walls.

The objective of the following exercise is to customize a curtain wall that is instance-based (meaning you will not define any type parameters yet). You will manually add curtain grids that will subdivide the wall into smaller panels. The last part of the exercise will be to add curtain mullions, which are hosted to the curtain grids, and manually space the grids to the desired width.

Exercise 2.7: Create and Customize a Curtain Wall

To begin, open the book's web page at www.sybex.com/go/revit2015essentials, download the files for chapter 2, and open the file c02-ex-2.7.start.rvt.

1. The starting file should open to the default 3D view. Select the Curtain Grid tool from the Build panel on the Architecture tab of the ribbon.

2. As you hover over the edge of the curtain wall, you are prompted with a dashed line that indicates where the grid will be placed. Also notice

that the dashed line should snap at the midpoint and at one-third lengths from either end of the curtain wall.

3. Using the default All Segments placement option on the ribbon, add three grid lines along the horizontal and vertical directions. At this point the curtain wall should look like Figure 2.18.

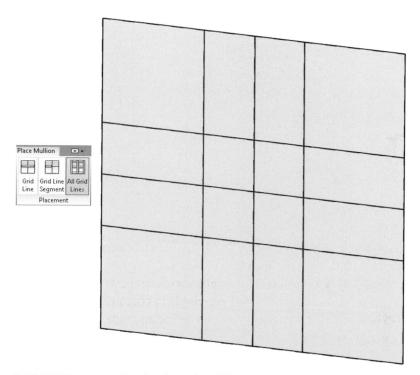

FIGURE 2.18 Completed curtain grid lines

4. Now that you've added curtain grids, you can add mullions to the curtain panel. Select the Mullion tool from the Build panel, and choose the All Grid Lines placement option on the ribbon (Figure 2.18).

5. Hover the cursor over any of the curtain grid lines, and they should all highlight, indicating where the mullions will be placed. Left-click and mullions will be assigned to all empty grid lines (in this example they should be added everywhere). Press the Esc key once to exit the command.

6. Move the cursor over one of the vertical mullions and press the Tab key until the curtain grid line is highlighted. The Tab key is important when working with curtain walls. Because there are several elements that potentially share a common edge (walls, panels, grids, and mullions), it is necessary to press and release the Tab key to toggle what will be selected (Figure 2.19).

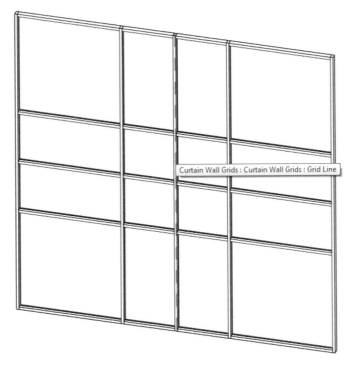

FIGURE 2.19 Mullions and selecting the grid line

7. Once the grid line is highlighted, left-click to select it.
   Once it is selected, two temporary dimensions should be visible.

8. Left-click the temporary dimension text; you can enter exact values to move the grid line to.

9. Set the vertical first and last grid lines to be 2′-0″ from the curtain wall edge. Leave the center grid line where it is. Set the horizontal first and last grid lines to be 3′-0″ from the curtain wall edge.

> Alternatively you can left-click+drag the curtain grid line to move it in a less precise manner.

When complete, the curtain wall should look like the one shown in Figure 2.20.

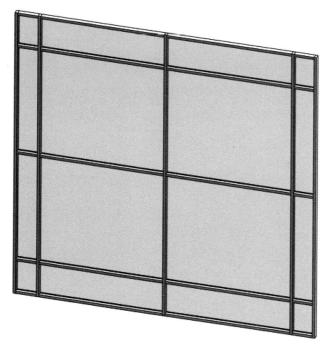

FIGURE 2.20 Final instance-based curtain wall

CURVED CURTAIN PANELS

Curved curtain-wall segments that you create will appear flat until you add the vertical grid lines. But specifying exact grid locations during the design process is often tedious—and difficult to correct. To help, you can create a design panel from a specially created wall that is very thin and transparent. Use this wall to figure out the design, and then swap it out for a curtain wall later. The wall can even have a pattern file associated to it that visually helps it to read as a curtain panel. You can find an example of this type of wall in c02-Curtain Walls.rvt (c02-Curtain Walls Metric.rvt), which is available with this chapter's exercise files.

In the previous exercise you were able to modify the curtain grids and hosted mullion locations using temporary dimensions, since the curtain type properties did not have any set spacing parameters. In the next exercise the objective is to set some type property values for spacing and mullion types.

Exercise 2.8: Modify Curtain Wall Type Properties

To begin, go to the book's web page at www.sybex.com/go/revit2015essentials, download the files for Chapter 2, and open the file c02-ex-2.8start.rvt.

1. The starting file should open the to the default 3D view. Select one of the two curtain walls and click Edit Type in the Properties palette.

2. Locate the Vertical Grid and Horizontal Grid settings for Layout (currently set to None). Set Vertical Grid Layout to Fixed Distance, Spacing 5'-0". Set Horizontal Grid Layout to Maximum Spacing, Spacing 4'-0". Click OK to close the Type Properties dialog.

3. Both curtain walls should update to show grid lines at the spacing you configured (Figure 2.21).

4. Select one of the curtain walls and click Edit Type again. Under Construction, set the Curtain Panel to System Panel : Solid. Then set the Join Condition to Border and Vertical Grid Continuous.

5. Scroll down further in the Type Properties dialog to locate the Vertical Mullions and Horizontal Mullions parameters. Set Interior Type for both Vertical and Horizontal Mullions to Rectangular Mullion : 2.5" 5" Rectangular. Do the same for the Border 1 Type and Border 2 Type, so all settings are using the same rectangular mullion. Click OK to close the Type Properties dialog, and both curtain walls should update (Figure 2.22).

   One condition you may notice is at the corner, where the two curtain walls meet. By default no corner mullion is specified, so the standard Rectangular Mullion : 2.5" 5" is used there for both overlapping ends. Corner mullions can be specified in the type properties under Border 1 or Border 2 Type.

   You can also override the mullions already placed in the model, which is more applicable at this condition since you do not want to update every border condition at every curtain wall instance for the entire model. When a curtain wall type contains defined spacing and mullions, you can still modify an individual segment by first using Unpin.

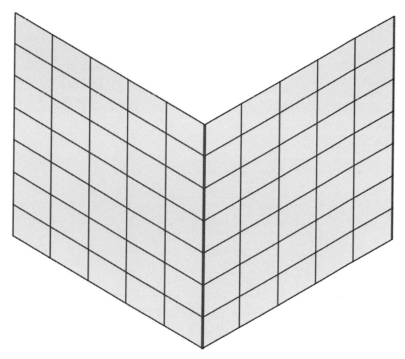

FIGURE 2.21   Curtain wall grids added

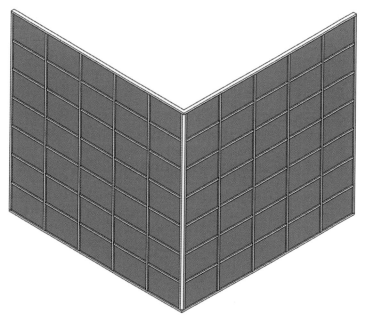

FIGURE 2.22   Curtain wall panels and mullions specified

6. From the 3D view hover the cursor over one of the border curtain mullions (it doesn't matter which you choose). Press the Tab key until the mullion is highlighted; then left-click to select it. While the mullion is selected, right-click and choose Select Mullions ➢ On Gridline. This will select every mullion on this last grid line (Figure 2.23).

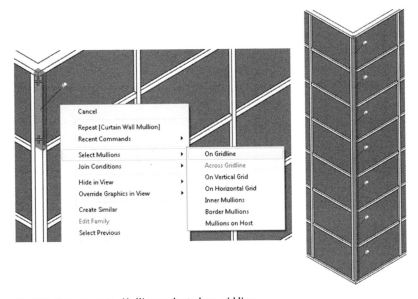

FIGURE 2.23 Mullions selected on grid line

7. Notice that the Properties palette shows the rectangular mullion type as grayed out. You can't simply swap it by default, because the type properties of the curtain wall define this type. In order to override the type, you need to first unpin the mullions. On the ribbon in the Modify panel click the Unpin tool.

8. Every curtain wall mullion on this grid line is now unpinned (and still selected). You don't need curtain mullions at both borders, so you can delete these. Since you unpinned them in the last step, you can simply press the Delete key.

9. Repeat step 6 to select the remaining border mullions along the grid line. Then use the Unpin tool again. For these you want to change the curtain mullion type from the Type Selector. Change the curtain wall mullions to L Corner Mullion : 5″ 5″ Corner. Now the corner condition should look similar to the one in Figure 2.24.

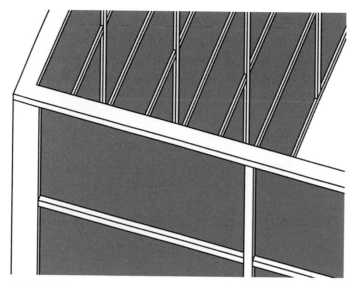

FIGURE 2.24 Curtain wall corner condition

Editing Wall Profiles

Basic, stacked, and curtain walls can have the standard rectangular shape modified to a custom shape using the Edit Profile tool. This tool is available on the ribbon after one wall is selected (it will be disabled if more than one wall is selected). When Edit Profile is activated (Figure 2.25), you can modify the rectangular profile of the wall by adding or modifying the existing sketch lines. Additionally, any closed-loop sketch lines you add in the interior will be considered openings when you click Finish Edit Mode.

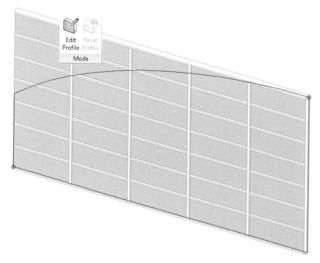

FIGURE 2.25 Edit wall profile

Embedding Curtain Walls

Curtain walls can also be embedded in walls. This may be useful for a custom storefront or similar conditions where you want the curtain wall to be hosted in a basic or stacked wall and the wall opening to be cut out automatically.

The objective of the following exercise is to add a curtain wall embedded in a basic wall. For the second portion of the exercise you will edit the embedded curtain wall profile to customize the shape.

Exercise 2.9: Embed and Edit Curtain Wall Profile

To begin, open the book's web page at www.sybex.com/go/revit2015essentials, download the files for Chapter 2, and open the file c02-ex-2.9.start.rvt.

1. The starting file should open to the Level 1 view. In this view there is a single basic brick wall.

2. From the Level 1 view, start the Wall tool and change the wall type to Curtain Wall : Storefront using the Type Selector.

3. Click Edit Type, and locate the Automatically Embed parameter. Confirm that it is checked (it should be by default). This parameter controls whether the curtain wall will automatically embed itself into a host wall.

4. Click OK to close the Type Properties dialog. Click anywhere over the brick wall in the Level 1 view. Click the second point 20'-0" from the first to add the curtain wall. Because Automatically Embed is checked, the curtain wall will be associated with the brick wall and the opening will be cut out of the wall.

5. Open the South Elevation view. Select the curtain wall, and from the Properties palette change the Base Offset parameter to 2'-0" (610 mm). Next, change the Unconnected Height parameter to 10'-0" (3050 mm) (Figure 2.26).

6. While still in the South Elevation view, select the embedded curtain wall. Click Edit Profile on the ribbon to enter sketch mode.

▶

For the curtain wall to be embedded into another wall it must be within 6 inches of the wall. It also must be parallel with the host wall.

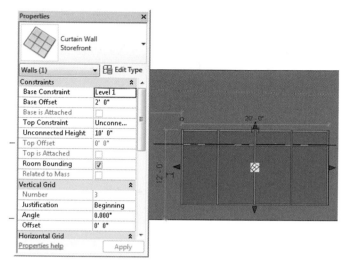

FIGURE 2.26 Curtain wall selected in wall

7. Select the top sketch line and press the Delete key to remove it. Then add a new sketch line, using the Start-End-Radius Arc draw tool. Click Finish Edit Mode to complete the sketch and update the curtain wall. Revit Architecture may warn you that some of the mullions in the original system can't be created. This is fine, because some of the mullions are outside the sketch area. Click Delete Element(s) to continue (Figure 2.27).

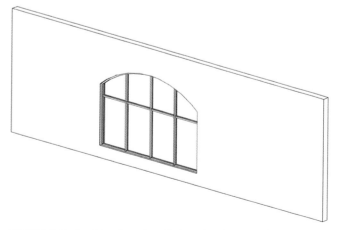

FIGURE 2.27 Curtain wall elevation view complete

The host wall will update around the embedded curtain wall to match the new profile defining the boundary condition.

Curtain Panels

Curtain panels are defined as part of the curtain wall type properties. Like the other curtain wall components, they can also be assigned on an instance basis or unpinned and changed to another infill type. A curtain panel can be a curtain panel family, a basic or stacked wall type, or another curtain wall.

Adding and Removing Grids and Mullions

So far in this chapter you have manually added curtain grids and curtain wall mullions, as well as defined the location for grid lines in the type properties. A typical curtain wall type in your project may have the majority of the grid spacing predefined by the type properties. However, you can still add or remove grid lines.

The objective of the following exercise is to manually add additional grid lines and curtain mullions to a curtain wall driven by type properties. In addition, you will remove some of the existing curtain grids to create a larger panel infill.

Then you will continue with a second exercise to modify some of the existing curtain panel instances in the curtain wall. As part of this exercise you will focus on adding a curtain panel door to the area where you removed grids and mullions.

Exercise 2.10: Add and Remove Curtain Grids and Mullions

To begin, open the book's web page at www.sybex.com/go/revit2015essentials, download the files for Chapter 2, and open the file c02-ex-2.10.start.rvt. This file will be used for this and the following exercise.

1. The starting file should open to the default 3D view. The curtain wall type Storefront - Door contains type properties for grid distances and mullion types.

2. Move the cursor over one of the vertical red mullions (colored for exercise identification), and press the Tab key until the curtain grid is highlighted.

3. On the ribbon notice that the Add/Remove Segments tool is now available. This tool appears only when curtain grids are selected. Click Add/Remove Segments and click the cursor over one of the

red mullions. It should remove the curtain grid as well as the curtain mullion since it is hosted on the grid.

4. The tool stays active so you can click the other vertical red curtain mullion to remove it. Repeat the steps to remove the remaining red horizontal curtain mullion, and you will end up with one panel, as highlighted in Figure 2.28.

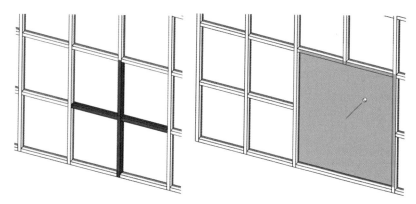

FIGURE 2.28 Removed curtain wall grids and mullions

5. You can also add curtain grids and mullions in addition to those defined in the type properties. Select the Curtain Grid tool from the Build panel on the Architecture tab of the ribbon. Change the Placement option to One Segment.

6. Add four vertical grid lines centered on the remaining lower curtain panels at 1′-8″ on each side. Notice that the rectangular mullions are automatically added, since the curtain wall type properties have this type specified for the Interior Type.

7. Select the four new vertical mullions (use the Ctrl key to add them to the same selection set) and use the Unpin tool. While they're still selected, change the curtain wall mullion to the 1″ Square type from the Type Selector (Figure 2.29).

8. Next, select the perpendicular curtain mullions above and below the new 1″ Square mullions (use the Ctrl key to add multiple items to the same selection set), and on the Mullion panel on the ribbon click Make Continuous (or click the Toggle Mullion Join symbol shown in Figure 2.30). This will toggle the mullion join at each location. The final model should look similar to Figure 2.30.

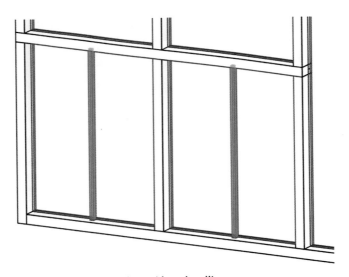

FIGURE 2.29 New grids and mullions

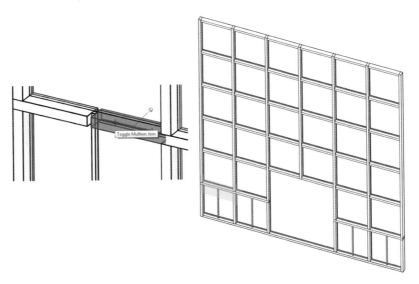

FIGURE 2.30 Finished mullions

Exercise 2.11: Customize Curtain Panels

To begin, open the book's web page at www.sybex.com/go/revit2015essentials, download the files for Chapter 2, and open the file c02-ex-2.11.start.rvt.

1. The starting file should open to the default 3D view. Select the lower eight curtain panels and click the Unpin tool. Change the curtain panel from System Panel Glazed to System Panel Solid.

2. Next, you want to add a door to the curtain wall in the largest panel. Select the large System Panel Glazed panel in the center and click Unpin. Change the panel to the Curtain Wall Dbl Glass panel from the Type Selector (Figure 2.31).

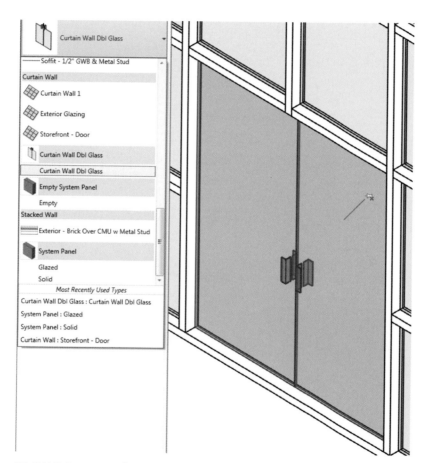

FIGURE 2.31 Curtain wall door condition

3. After adding the door, select the lower vertical curtain wall mullions on either side of the door (there are two mullions on each side) and toggle the mullion join to Make Continuous. This will extend the curtain mullions to the base of the curtain wall (first image in Figure 2.32).

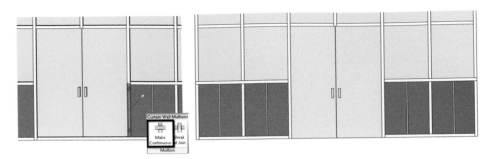

F I G U R E 2 . 3 2   Final curtain wall

4. Next, remove the rectangular curtain wall mullions directly under the Curtain Wall Dbl Glass panel. Select both pinned curtain wall mullions (in the same selection set) and use the Unpin tool. Once they're unpinned, you can press the Delete key to remove the curtain mullions (second image in Figure 2.32).

5. Notice that the curtain panel door adjusts to fill in the additional space after the mullions are deleted. If at any point you need to revert panel or mullion overrides, using the Pin tool will switch them back to the type defined in the curtain wall type properties.

Now You Know

Walls in Revit Architecture are flexible enough to support the initial conceptual design process all the way through the final iteration of a specific wall type. This flexibility is evident through the numerous techniques we have discussed to edit, manipulate, and build various wall configurations.

In this chapter, you learned about the different wall types and the relevant parameters. You created walls using a variety of different tools and methods. You further modified walls by hosting other objects such as doors, and you adjusted the profile and shape of the walls. In this chapter you also worked through a variety of exercises specific to curtain walls covering parameters, grids, mullions, and panels.

CHAPTER 3

Floors, Roofs, and Ceilings

This chapter will walk you through the most common horizontal host objects that make up your building. Although the process of creating a floor, roof, or ceiling is somewhat different for each, the tools used to edit each initial design element are similar and have overlapping methodology.

In this chapter, you'll learn to:

▶ **Create floors by sketching, editing, and picking**

▶ **Create sloped floors**

▶ **Create and modify a roof by footprint**

▶ **Create and modify a roof by extrusion**

▶ **Adjust the slope of a roof**

▶ **Create ceilings**

▶ **Create custom ceilings by sketching**

▶ **Add lights to a ceiling**

▶ **Slope and modify the ceiling type**

Creating Floors

There are quite a few ways to create floors in the Autodesk® Revit® Architecture software. The main objective for this chapter is to understand what the various approaches to a single floor type will do and what kind of relationships they'll make.

The objective of the following exercise is to first create floors by sketching the desired shape. Then, for the second part of the exercise you will use the Pick Wall tool to define the floor boundary.

Exercise 3.1: Create a Floor by Sketch and Pick Walls

To begin, go to the book's web page at www.sybex.com/go/revit2015essentials, download the files for Chapter 3, and open the file c03-ex-3.1start.rvt.

1. Open the Level 1 floor plan view. Select the Floor tool on the Build panel of the Architecture tab.

2. Revit will automatically enter sketch mode, which will allow you to create a sketch to define the boundary of your floor.

3. Create a simple sketch for the floor, 15′ × 30″ (4500 mm × 9000 mm). The dimensions are for reference only; even though this is a simple shape, what's more important is how you can manipulate the shape.

4. Confirm that the floor type is Generic – 12″ (Generic – 300 mm) in the Type Selector. Finish the sketch, and open your default 3D view. Your floor should resemble the one shown in Figure 3.1.

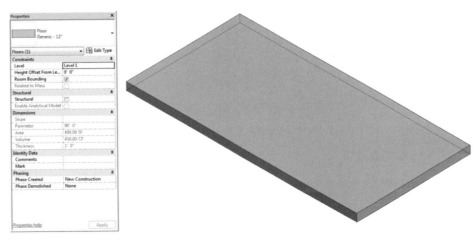

F I G U R E 3 . 1   The finished floor by sketching

5. Next, you will create a floor by picking walls. Open the Level 1 view and select the Floor tool on the Build panel of the Architecture tab to enter sketch mode. Select the Pick Walls tool from the Draw palette. Doing so allows you to select an individual wall or an entire chain of walls.

6. Move the cursor over one of the wall edges to the right and then press and release the Tab key. Your selection cycles from one wall to the series of walls. When all of the walls highlight, select them with one pick.

7. In the Properties palette set the Height Offset From Level parameter to 0″ (0 mm). Click Finish Edit Mode to exit the sketch. Select and move some of the walls that were used to determine the floor sketch. Notice that the boundary of the floor automatically updates (Figure 3.2). This is incredibly powerful for a multistory building, where updating one floor at a time would be nearly impossible.

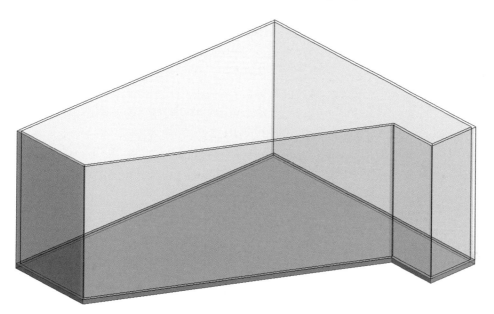

FIGURE 3.2 The finished floor by picking walls

Note that the edge of the new floor is constructed where you click your mouse when you pick the wall in reference to the interior or exterior of the wall. The floor goes to the outside of the wall; to do that, you have to pick the outside edge of the wall — otherwise, the floor aligns with the interior. The entire chain of sketch lines is created that corresponds to all the walls.

EXTEND INTO WALL (TO CORE)

When using the Pick Walls tool, there is a setting on the Options Bar called Extend into wall (to core). By default, when you pick a compound wall with multiple layers, the floor sketch will extend to the core boundary of the wall. If desired, you can specify an offset using a positive or negative value. If this option is unchecked, the floor sketch will use the outer interior or exterior face of the wall.

Exercise 3.2: Edit the Floor Boundary

The objective of the following exercise is to edit and modify an existing floor boundary. To begin, go to the book's web page at www.sybex.com/go/revit2015essentials, download the files for Chapter 3, and open the file c03-ex-3.2start.rvt.

1. Open the Level 1 floor plan view, select the floor, and click Edit Boundary from the Modify Floors contextual tab.

2. Add additional sketch lines to generate the shape at the lower right in Figure 3.3. Don't forget to trim back any intersecting lines.

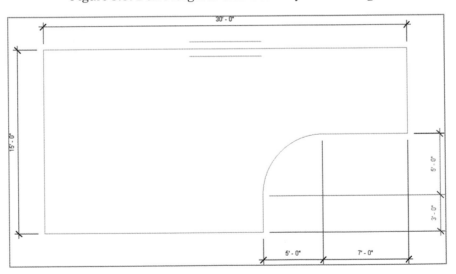

FIGURE 3.3 Modifying the floor sketch

3. Finish the sketch by clicking Finish Edit Mode. Select the floor, and notice that the options and dimension properties have already updated, as shown in Figure 3.4.

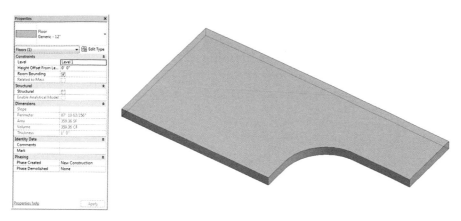

F I G U R E 3 . 4 The modified floor

4. Create another floor of the same type and same initial dimensions, 15′ × 30′ (4500 mm × 9000 mm), near the first floor (reference Figure 3.5 for the location). Leave some space between the two floors.

5. Offset the floor 1′-0″ (300 mm) above Level 1 by entering this value into Height Offset From Level in the Properties palette.

6. Finish the sketch to complete the floor (Figure 3.5).

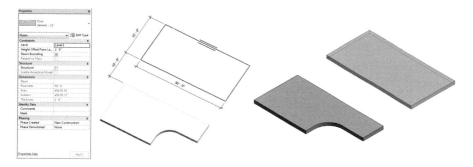

F I G U R E 3 . 5 New floor 1′-0″ (300 mm) above Level 1

Not all floors are flat, and Revit Architecture has several tools to create sloped conditions. In the following exercise you will investigate both options by creating and modifying sloped floors using two tools: Slope Arrow and Shape Editing.

Exercise 3.3: Create Sloped Floors

To begin, go to the book's web page at www.sybex.com/go/revit2015essentials, download the files for Chapter 3, and open the file c03-ex-3.3start.rvt.

7. Now that you've added the proper locations to break the slope, you need to modify the points at the ends of the lines to change the slope of the floor. Start by returning to your default 3D view. As you hover over the endpoint of the line, Revit Architecture highlights the shape handles. Press the Tab key to highlight a specific handle, and then select it (Figure 3.10).

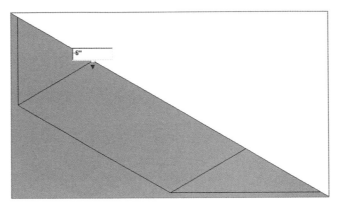

F I G U R E 3 . 1 0   Editing the shape handle

8. Adjust the elevation of the shape handle as shown in Figure 3.10. In this case, you're depressing the floor, so the value must be negative. But you could also increase the elevation in a small area by using a positive value.

9. Do the same for the shape handle to the right. When you've finished, the depressed area resembles Figure 3.11.

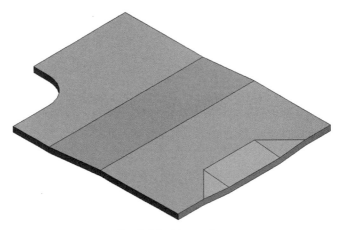

F I G U R E 3 . 1 1   The finished depression

For the occasional or irregular opening in a floor, it's easy to add an opening using the Opening tools. For openings that occur from level to level and are vertically repetitive (such as a shaft or an elevator core), you can use the Shaft tool. This tool allows you to create openings in numerous floors, roofs, and ceilings quickly and easily.

The objective of the following two exercises is to create openings in your floor objects. The first exercise will focus on the Opening By Face tool. The second exercise will focus on the Shaft Opening tool.

Exercise 3.4: Create an Opening with the Opening by Face Tool

To begin, go to the book's web page at www.sybex.com/go/revit2015essentials, download the files for Chapter 3, and open the file c03-ex-3.4start.rvt.

1. From the Architecture tab on the ribbon, select the Opening By Face tool on the Opening panel.

2. Select any edge of the sloped floor you created to initiate sketch mode.

3. Sketch an opening 10′ × 3′ (3000 mm × 1000 mm) in the center floor panel. There's no limit to the number of interior sketches you can create.

4. Click Finish Edit Mode to complete the sketch. The result resembles Figure 3.12.

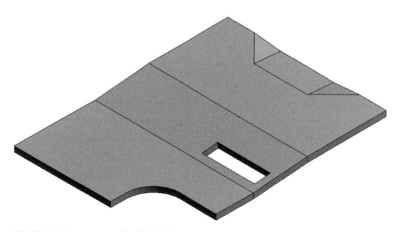

FIGURE 3.12 The finished opening

5. Return to the Level 1 view, and select the Shaft Opening tool from the Opening panel.

6. Create a new 20′ × 3′ (6100 mm × 1000 mm) rectangle perpendicular to the last two you drew.

7. Confirm that the Top Constraint is set to Level 10 so the shaft goes up to the top floor. Then set the Top Offset to a minimum of 1′ (300 mm) to ensure it fully cuts the floor. A higher value can be specified as needed.

8. Be certain to assign a Base Offset value of -1′ (-300 mm), because the upper floor is slightly above the level (Figure 3.15).

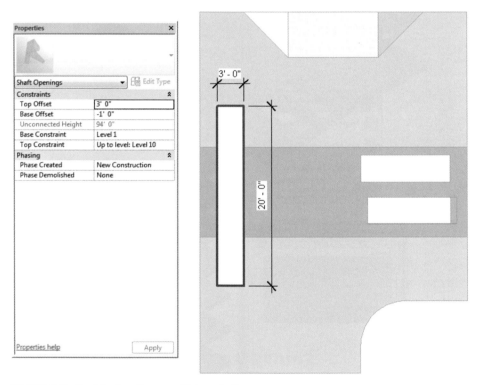

F I G U R E 3 . 1 5 Creating a multistory shaft

Figure 3.16 shows the resulting shaft in 3D. All the floors were cut automatically. Any ceilings, roofs, and additional floors created later that are between the same levels will be cut automatically as well.

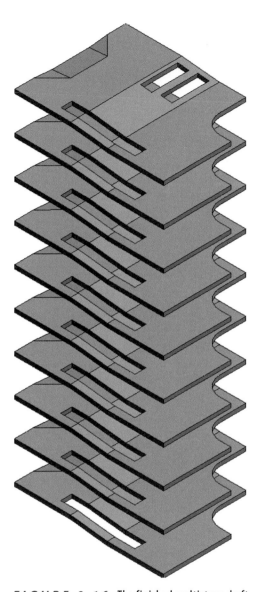

FIGURE 3.16 The finished multistory shaft

Creating Roofs

There are two primary methods for creating roofs, which you will explore in this chapter: Roof by Footprint and Roof by Extrusion. You create a Roof by Footprint roof much like you do floors: from a sketch resulting from either drawn lines or picked walls. And as with floors, if you pick the exterior walls as a reference, then moving the walls will move the corresponding edges of the roof. Roofs can be created in elevation using the Roof by Extrusion tool, which we will cover in the second exercise.

The objective of the following exercise is to create a roof by picking the outline of existing walls.

Exercise 3.6: Create a Roof by Footprint

To begin, go to the book's web page at www.sybex.com/go/revit2015essentials, download the files for Chapter 3, and open the file c03-ex-3.6start.rvt.

1. Open the Level 1 plan view. Select the Roof by Footprint command from the Roof flyout on the Architecture tab. At this point, Revit Architecture automatically asks you to select the level with which this roof is associated.

2. Select Level 3. Don't worry; you can change the level at any time later.

   Again, you don't have to pick all the walls individually or sketch all the roof boundary lines.

3. Select the Pick Walls option on the Draw panel of the Modify | Create Roof Footprint tab. Uncheck the Defines slope setting on the Options Bar.

4. Move the cursor over one of the exterior walls and press the Tab key until the entire chain is highlighted; then left-click. All the roof boundary lines will be created.

5. Because this will be a sloped roof, you can make the slope perpendicular to the left edge by checking the Defines Slope box on the Options Bar or the Properties palette.

6. Define the Slope property for this roof sketch line with a 1″ / 12″ (83 mm / 1000 mm) rise over run (Figure 3.17).

Note the icon with double arrows on the sketch lines for the roof: clicking it flips the boundary lines to the inside or outside of the wall face. Click this icon to move all the boundary lines to the inside of the wall's faces.

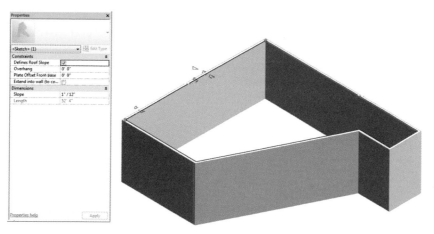

FIGURE 3.17 Roof sketch and slope properties

7. Finish the sketch, and look at the project in 3D.

   Although the roof begins at Level 3 and has the proper slope, it's immediately obvious that the walls don't extend up to the roof.

8. To resolve this condition select all the walls (using the Tab key to select the entire chain), and set Top Constraint to Level 4 in the Properties palette. The results resemble Figure 3.18.

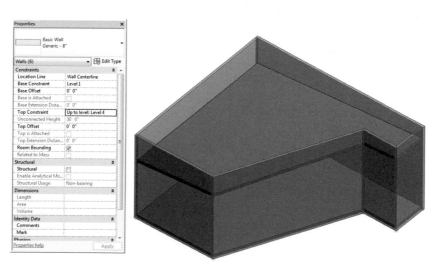

FIGURE 3.18 Adjusting the wall height

The objective of the following exercise is to create an extruded roof and join it to an existing roof.

Exercise 3.7: Create a Roof by Extrusion

To begin, go to the book's web page at www.sybex.com/go/revit2015essentials, download the files for Chapter 3, and open the file c03-ex-3.7start.rvt.

1. Select the Roof by Extrusion command from the Roof flyout on the Architecture tab. The Work Plane dialog should prompt you to specify a new work plane. Choose the Pick a plane option and select the roof face highlighted in Figure 3.19.

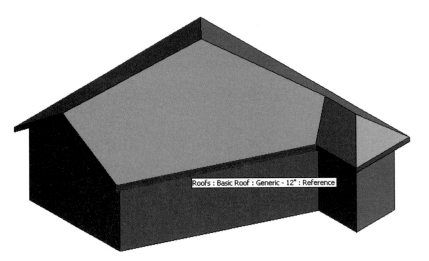

Roofs : Basic Roof : Generic - 12" : Reference

FIGURE 3.19 Selecting the roof face

2. You're prompted to associate the roof to the appropriate level. This step is important for scheduling purposes; you can modify the value later. For now, select Level 3 because it's closest to the base of the extruded roof.

3. Next, you'll create the sketch for the extruded roof. The sketch line isn't a closed loop: It's just a line (or series of connected lines) that defines the top of the extruded roof. For this example, you'll create an arc. Select any of the Arc tools from the Draw panel.

4. Create the arc approximately as shown in Figure 3.20. When you've finished drawing the arc, set Extrusion End in the Properties palette to **20'-0"** (6100 mm).

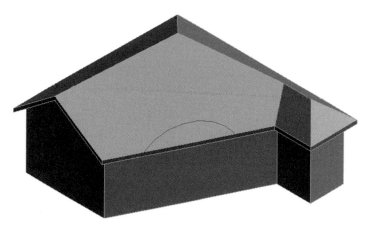

FIGURE 3.20 Creating the arc

5. Finish the sketch. The roof springs from the arc you created, but it's not reaching back and connecting to the roof face. This issue is easy to resolve.

6. Select the roof extrusion, and then select the Join/Unjoin Roof tool on the Geometry panel.

7. Hover over the rear edge of the extruded roof, as shown in the left image of Figure 3.21.

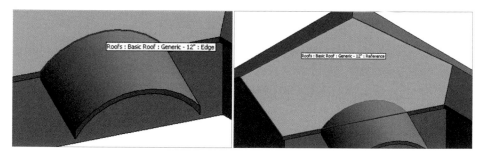

FIGURE 3.21 Attaching the roof

8. Select the face of the previously created roof that you want to connect to the extruded roof. The extruded roof now extends back to meet the face of the other roof (Figure 3.22). If either roof is modified, Revit Architecture will do its best to maintain this connected relationship.

7. Make sure Height Offset is the same for both tails and both heads. Finish the sketch. The results resemble the roof in Figure 3.24.

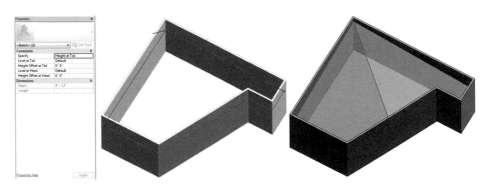

FIGURE 3.24 Roof created from two slope arrows

The objective of the following exercise is to create multiple slopes that are perpendicular to the edges using the Defines Slope option.

Exercise 3.9: Create Multiple Roof Slopes

To begin, go to the book's web page at www.sybex.com/go/ revit2015essentials, download the files for Chapter 3, and open the file c03-ex-3.9start.rvt.

1. Select the roof and click Edit Footprint to reenter sketch mode for the roof. Delete both slope arrows.

2. Select all the lines that represent the roof sketch. You can do this by holding down Ctrl and selecting the lines individually or by clicking one line and pressing Tab to select the rest of the lines.

3. With the lines selected, in the Options Bar enter 3′ (1000 mm) for the overhang. The overhang direction will move positive in relation to the side of the wall picked (exterior or interior). Positive or negative dimensions can be entered if the sketch moves in the opposite direction. Also keep in mind that the Overhang option is available only for roof sketch lines created using the Pick Walls option.

4. Select the Defines Roof Slope option for all the boundary edges from the Properties palette. Also modify the Slope property for a slope of 9″ / 12″ (750 mm / 1000 mm). The roof should look like Figure 3.25.

FIGURE 3.25 Offsetting the roof sketch and defining slopes

5. Finish the sketch. Initially, the edges of the wall extend beyond the overhang of the roof. Select all the exterior walls (use the Tab key), and then select the Attach Top/Base option on the Modify | Walls tab. Click the roof to attach it, and the result resembles Figure 3.26.

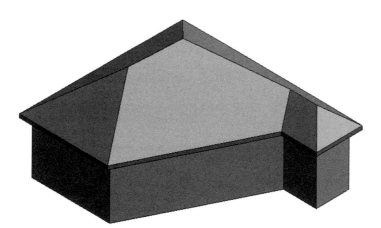

FIGURE 3.26 Attaching the walls to the roof

6. The great thing about attaching walls is that if the roof's angle or slopes change, the walls will automatically react to the new condition. To test this, select the roof and click Edit Footprint to reenter sketch mode. Remove the Defines Slope option for one of the edges.

4. Select the Ceiling tool on the Architecture tab, and pick inside the rooms shown in Figure 3.29 to automatically place the ceilings. Notice that Revit Architecture centers the grid based on the space you've selected.

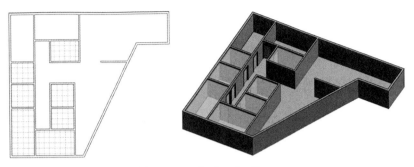

FIGURE 3.29   Resulting automatic placed ceilings

5. Next, you'll place ceilings in the upper-left corner of the ceiling plan for Level 1, but this time you'll share the ceiling between the two spaces. This practice is common in interior projects. The partitions extend only to the underside of the ceiling (rather than connect to the structure above). Select Sketch Ceiling on the Ceiling panel of the Modify | Place Ceiling tab. Add sketch lines as shown in the first image in Figure 3.30. The result is shown in the second image.

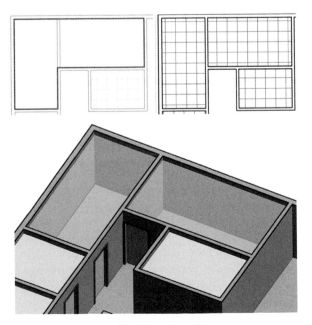

FIGURE 3.30   Sketching the ceiling

6. Create another ceiling using Sketch Ceiling in the upper-right area of the plan (Figure 3.31). Choose the 2′ × 4′ (600 mm × 1200 mm) system from the Type Selector before you finish the sketch of the ceiling.

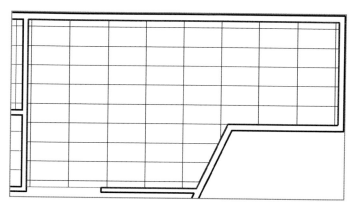

FIGURE 3.31   A 2′ × 4′ (600 mm × 1200 mm) ceiling

7. Create a GWB on Mtl. Stud Ceiling for the area shown in Figure 3.32.

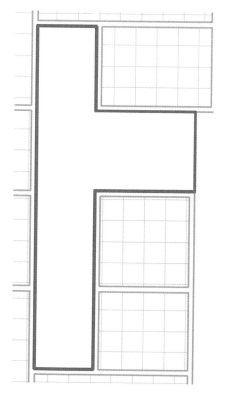

FIGURE 3.32   Creating a GWB On Mtl. Stud Ceiling

4. Click Finish Edit Mode.

5. To get a better idea of the finished configuration in 3D, go to a 3D view and orient a section box of the Level 1 plan view.

6. Right-click the ViewCube, and from the Floor Plans flyout of the context menu, select Level 1.

7. Orbit the view or use the ViewCube to choose the desired angle.

8. Use the grip arrows to pull the boundaries of the section box to resemble Figure 3.36. You'll find that working this way is helpful because having both 2D and 3D views aids in communicating any design issues.

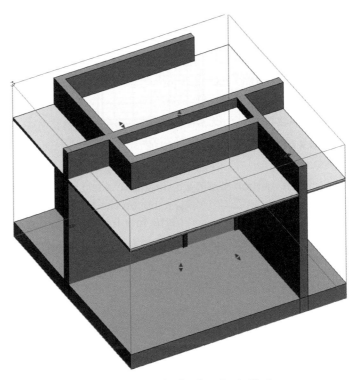

F I G U R E   3 . 3 6   Final section box location in 3D view

The objective of the following exercise is to add light fixtures hosted to the ceiling. Then for the second part of the exercise you will rotate the ceiling grid.

Exercise 3.12: Add Lights and Rotate the Grid

To begin, go to the book's web page at www.sybex.com/go/revit2015essentials, download the files for Chapter 3, and open the file c03-ex-3.12start.rvt.

1. On the Insert tab, select Load Family on the Load From Library panel.

2. Browse and open the Lighting\Architectural\Internal folder, and double-click the family Ceiling Light - Linear Box.rfa (M_Ceiling Light - Linear Box.rfa).

3. Click the Place a Component button, and the ceiling light family should be the default.

4. Select the 2′ × 4′ (2 Lamp) - 120V (0600 mm × 1200 mm) type from the Type Selector. You'll place lighting fixtures into the 2′ × 4′ (0600 mm × 1200 mm) ceiling in the upper-right ceiling plan.

5. The insertion point for the light is the center of the light. Place the first light, and then use the Align tool to move it into the right spot.

6. Use the Copy tool on the Modify panel to copy the first light based on the intersection of the ceiling grid. All the lights are shown in Figure 3.37.

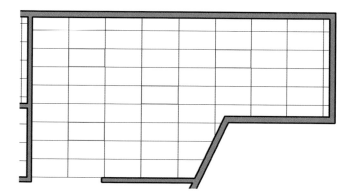

FIGURE 3.37 Placing lights

7. To rotate the grid, select any grid line, and use the Rotate tool on the Modify panel to rotate it. In this case, specify a 10-degree angle. Notice that the lights rotate as well.

8. Click and drag the ceiling grid lines to better center the lights in the overall space. Again, the lights move with the grid. The Move, Align, and Rotate tools are all available to modify ceilings when a grid line is selected.

    This technique is incredibly helpful for maintaining design coordination. The finished condition is shown on the right in Figure 3.38.

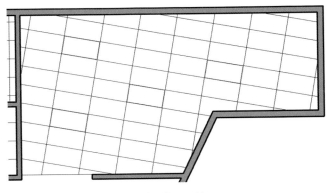

FIGURE 3.38   Rotated ceiling grid

The objective of the following exercise is to slope the ceiling by placing a slope arrow while editing the boundary of the ceiling. You will also change the ceiling type during this exercise.

Exercise 3.13: Slope the Ceiling

To begin, go to the book's web page at www.sybex.com/go/revit2015essentials, download the files for Chapter 3, and open the file c03-ex-3.13start.rvt.

1. First, select the ceiling and using the Type Selector in the Properties palette change the ceiling type to GWB on Mtl. Stud. Notice that the ceiling updates to reflect the new ceiling type.

2. Select the edge of the ceiling, and choose Edit Boundary on the Mode panel on the Modify | Ceilings tab.

3. Place a slope arrow as shown in the top image in Figure 3.39. Set the Height Offset values for the Tail and Head to 0′-0″ and 3′-0″ (1000 mm), respectively.

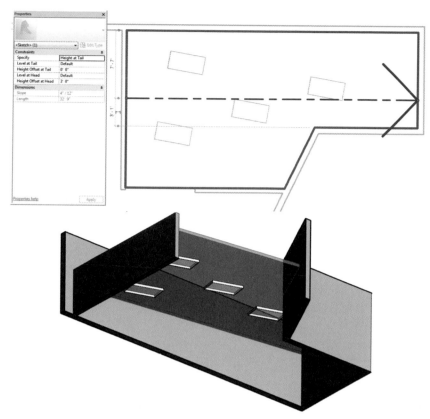

FIGURE 3.39 Adding a slope arrow to the ceiling

4. Finish the sketch. The result (bottom image in Figure 3.39) is shown in 3D using a section box. The lights should follow the revised ceiling slope.

Now You Know

Floors, roofs, and ceilings in Revit Architecture are very different object types that share a relatively common set of modification tools. You have the flexibility to create a set of objects and come back to them when additional information is known or the design intent changes. Revit makes it easy to swap types, edit the boundary, or revert to the original condition with a consistent set of modification tools.

In this chapter, you learned about creating floors and later modifying the floor to add openings, change the boundary, or add slope. You learned about the different methods to create roofs and later modifying the roof slope to create varying conditions. And lastly you learned about creating ceilings and then modifying the ceiling boundary, type, and hosting light fixtures.

CHAPTER 4

Stairs, Ramps, and Railings

Autodesk® Revit® Architecture software contains powerful tools for creating stairs, railings, and ramps. These elements are created and controlled with separate tools, which we will discuss and utilize in this chapter. In addition, these separate elements can interact with each other to form more complex systems, which we will also cover during the exercises in this chapter.

In this chapter, you'll learn to:

▶ **Create and modify railings**

▶ **Create stairs by component**

▶ **Create stairs by sketch**

▶ **Customize stair landings**

▶ **Create multistory stairs**

▶ **Create and customize ramps**

Creating a Generic Railing

Stairs contain numerous parameters, but not all of the parameter controls are equally important during the design process. Design is often about the intent of what something is as well as where it is meant to go. Once the intent is resolved, it's necessary to go back and revise the specifics of how something will be carefully assembled or to add additional detail when known.

Because the tools for railings, stairs, and ramps are somewhat separate, you'll begin the exercises by first creating a simplified railing. This way, when you create a series of stair configurations, you'll have a new, default railing to apply to each of them.

In the following exercise you will create a railing and edit the various
properties and components that make up the railing tool.

Exercise 4.1: Create a Generic Railing

To begin, go to the book's web page at www.sybex.com/go/revit2015essentials,
download the files for Chapter 4, and open the file c04-ex-4.1start.rvt.

1. Open the default 3D view by selecting the small house icon on the
   Quick Access toolbar (QAT) ⌂. Select the Architecture tab, and
   choose the Railing flyout from the Circulation panel. Select the
   Sketch Path option to enter sketch mode.
   Before you draw a railing, you'll create a new type.

2. Select Edit Type from the Properties palette, and with the
   Type Handrail – Rectangular current, click Duplicate in the Type
   Properties dialog box. Name the new railing **Handrail – Design**, and
   click OK twice to exit all the dialog boxes.

3. Draw a path line 30′ (10000 mm) long.
   This line will define your railing path.

4. Click Finish Edit Mode to exit the sketch, which will create the railing.
   This will be the default rail in the exercise file (Figure 4.1).

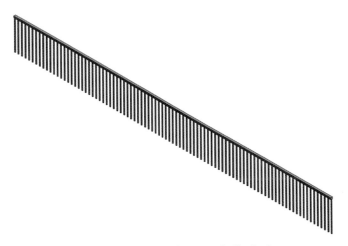

FIGURE 4.1 The default railing: Handrail – Design

Next, you will edit some of the newly created railing properties.

5. Select the railing, and choose Edit Type from the Properties palette to open the Type Properties dialog, as shown in Figure 4.2.

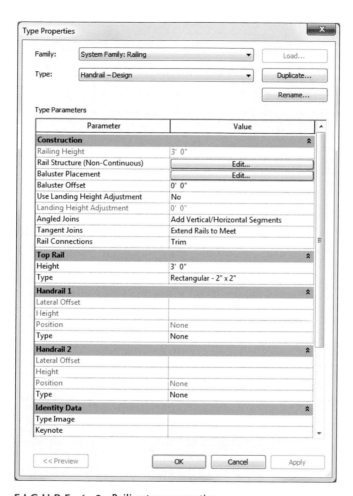

FIGURE 4.2   Railing type properties

6. Click Edit for the Rail Structure (Non-Continuous) parameter. In the resulting dialog box click Insert. This will add another rail to your railing type. In the Name field enter **Low Rail**. Set the Height to 1'-0" (300 mm) and change the Profile to Rectangular Handrail : 2" × 2" (Rectangular - 50 × 50 mm) (Figure 4.3). Close the dialog box by clicking OK to return to the Type Properties dialog.

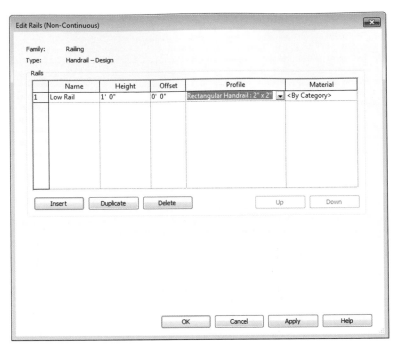

FIGURE 4.3 Edit Rails dialog box

7. Locate the Top Rail group. Set the Height to 3'-6" (**1060** mm). Leave the Type as Rectangular - 2" × 2" (Rectangular - 50 × 50 mm). This parameter controls the top rail used in the railing.

    Next, you will modify the balusters.

8. In the Type Properties dialog box, click the Edit button for the Baluster Placement parameter.

9. In the resulting dialog box, find the Main Pattern panel, select the second line (Regular Baluster), and set its Baluster Family value to Baluster - Square : 1" (Baluster - Square : 25 mm). Set the Dist. From Previous parameter to 5" (**125** mm).

10. In the Posts area, set the Baluster Family value for the Start Post, Corner Post, and End Post parameters to None (as shown in Figure 4.4).

11. Click OK to close the Edit Baluster Placement dialog box, and click OK again to close the Type Properties dialog box.

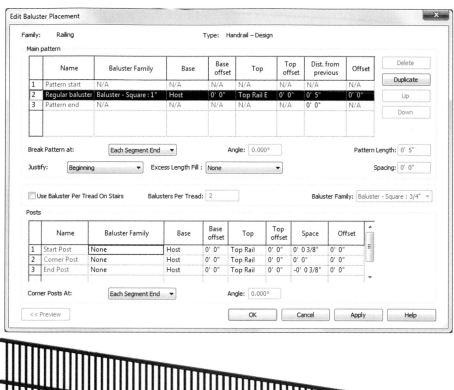

FIGURE 4.4 Baluster settings and completed railing

Creating Stair Configurations

Revit Architecture has two stair tools: Stair by Component and Stair by Sketch. The tools are located on the Architecture tab on the Circulation panel. The more recent stair tool is Stair by Component. As the name suggests, this tool will help you create stairs that can be broken down into their individual components for easier manipulation. This is the default stair tool on the ribbon in Revit Architecture. The original stair tool, Stair by Sketch, is located in the Stair flyout. The majority of our exercises in this chapter will focus on the more recent Stair by Component tool.

The resulting stair is shown in the default 3D view in Figure 4.8.

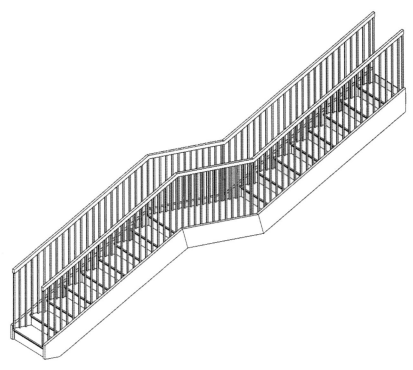

FIGURE 4.8　The resulting stair with railing

Now you'll create a second component stair to adjust some additional parameters.

5. Start the Stair By Component tool again, but before you pick a point to start the first run, choose the Location Line option from the Options Bar.

6. Set the Location Line to Exterior Support: Left. This will align the outside edge of the stair with your pick points, making it easier to snap to existing geometry.

7. For the start of the first run, click the endpoint of reference plane 1 where it meets the wall. Move to the right 6'-5" (955 mm), and click again to complete this run.

Each stair run component can have its own width using the Actual Run Width parameter on the Options Bar or Properties palette. You can enter this value either before or after placement.

8. Start the second stair run using the same Location Line setting, and click at the endpoint of reference plane 2 where it meets the wall. Move down anywhere past 9′-0″ (2750 mm), and click the last point to complete the second run (Figure 4.9).

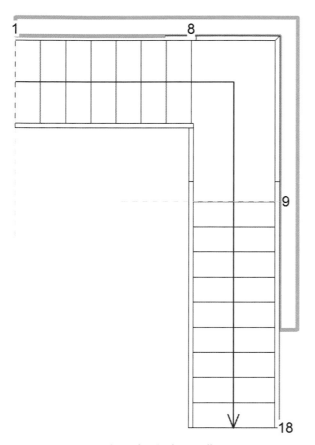

FIGURE 4.9 Second stair along wall

One of the nice features of component stairs is the ability to dynamically change the stair using shape handles.

9. Select the landing that was automatically created and notice the shape handles. Drag the landing edge shape handle down any distance to enlarge the landing. Notice that the stair run automatically moves down to reflect the new landing size.

8. Click Edit Type to open the stair Type Properties.

9. Under Risers, uncheck the End With Riser parameter and click OK to close the dialog.

This will remove the riser that is generated at the end of the stair.

10. Click Finish Edit Mode to complete the stair.

Ignore any warnings received about actual number of risers created.

11. Select the two railings that were automatically created, and swap the type in the Type Selector to Glass Panel - Bottom Fill. The completed stair is shown in Figure 4.14.

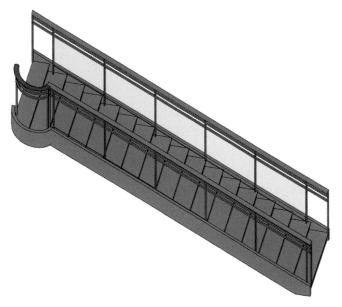

FIGURE 4.14 Completed sketch-based stair

In the following exercise you will customize an existing Stair by Component landing to reflect changes to the design.

Exercise 4.4: Customize and Create a Component Stair Landing

To begin, go to the book's web page at www.sybex.com/go/revit2015essentials, download the files for Chapter 4, and open the file c04-ex-4.4start.rvt.

1. From the Level 1 plan view, select the existing stair and click Edit Stairs to enter edit mode.

2. Click to select the existing landing object.
   You want to customize the landing shape so you will need to convert the landing to a sketch.

3. Click Convert To Sketch-Based on the Tools panel. Close the dialog confirming that this conversion is irreversible.

4. Notice there is a new option called Edit Sketch on the same Tools panel.

5. Click Edit Sketch to edit the landing boundary. Select and delete the existing landing boundary line (the longest line closest to the wall).

6. Set the type of lines to Boundary in the Draw panel. Set the draw mode to Pick Lines. Set the Options Bar Offset parameter to 2″ (50 mm) so you can compensate for your support distance along the wall.

7. Pick the faces of the interior wall lines to create the new landing sketch lines. Use the Trim/Extend To Corner tool to clean up the new boundary lines.

8. For the last segment, at the start of the second stair run you will need to create a small sketch line with the same 2″ (50 mm) offset. This offset will accommodate the stringers that will be created around the landing.
   The final sketch is shown in Figure 4.15.

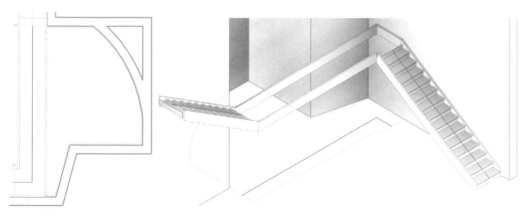

FIGURE 4.15 Revised landing sketch

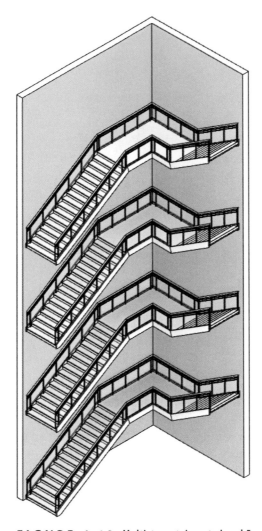

FIGURE 4.18 Multistory stair up to Level 5

Revit will repeat the stair up to the level you specified, including any railings that are currently attached to the stair.

4. Select one of the railings and notice that all four instances of the railing are selected.

5. Change the railing type to Guardrail - Pipe and notice that all four railings update to reflect the type change.

6. Select the stair and click Edit Stairs to enter edit mode.

7. Open the Level 1 floor plan view. Select the landing, and using the shape handles adjust it to be 2-6″ (760 mm) on each side that meets the run (Figure 4.19).

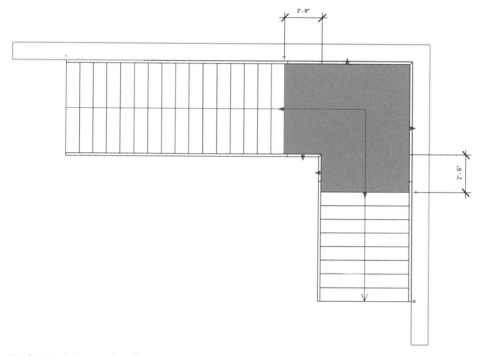

FIGURE 4.19 Landing adjustment

8. Click Finish Edit Mode to return to the project.

9. Open the 3D view again, and notice that every stair landing has also been updated.

10. Select the stair and change the Multistory Top Level parameter to Level 4.

   The stair will update to reflect the new top-level assignment (Figure 4.20).

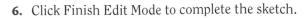

6. Click Finish Edit Mode to complete the sketch.

7. Open the default 3D view and note that the railings are not yet hosted to the stair but are instead hosted to Level 1.

8. Select one of the railings and click Pick New Host on the Tools panel.

9. Click the stair; this will change the railing host from Level 1 to instead attach and follow the geometry of the stair.

10. Click Pick New Host for the second railing to complete the new railing host (Figure 4.23).

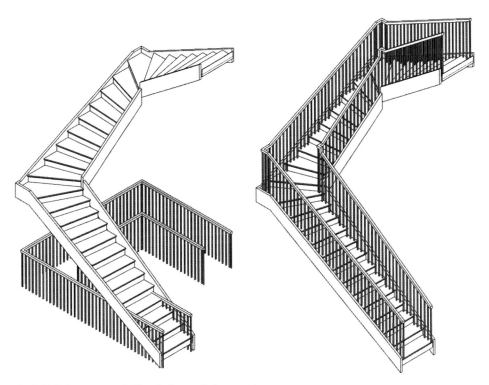

FIGURE 4.23 Railing before and after new host

In the following exercise you will customize an existing railing top rail to allow for a custom termination condition.

Exercise 4.7: Edit Railing Top Rail and Slope

To begin, go to the book's web page at www.sybex.com/go/revit2015essentials, download the files for Chapter 4, and open the file c04-ex-4.7start.rvt.

1. Open the example file to the 3D view.

2. Move the cursor over the top rectangular rail and press the Tab key once. The top rail should be highlighted.

3. Click to select the top rail (Figure 4.24).

4. Once it's selected, click Edit Rail on the Continuous Rail panel.

FIGURE 4.24 Select the top rail.

5. Click Edit Path and choose the Line Draw shape.

6. Draw a custom path for the top rail starting at the endpoint of the existing path, similar to Figure 4.25.

Edit
Path

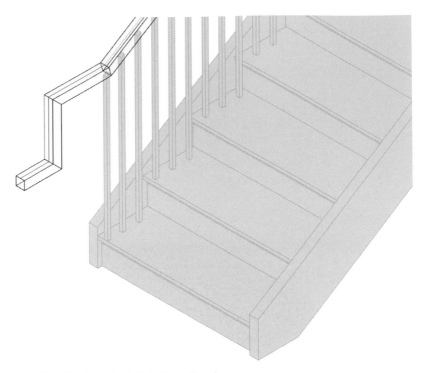

FIGURE 4.25 Updated top rail path

7. Click Finish Edit Mode twice to finish editing the top rail and return to the project.

   Next, you'll correct the railing condition at the top of the landing to match the flat slope.

8. Open the Level 1 floor plan view.

9. Select the railing and click Edit Path to return to sketch mode.

10. Use the Modify panel's Split Element tool ⊕ to split the railing path at the edge of the landing (Figure 4.26).

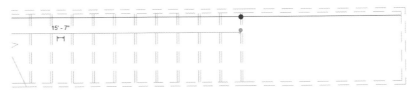

FIGURE 4.26 Split railing path sketch

11. Press the Esc key twice, and select the split railing sketch path over the landing.

12. On the Options Bar change the Slope to Flat.

13. Click Finish Edit Mode to exit the railing sketch.

14. Open the default 3D view, and notice that the railing condition is now flat over the landing.

    You can use the Slope controls for railing conditions when you need to override how the default slope will be calculated. The completed railing is shown in Figure 4.27.

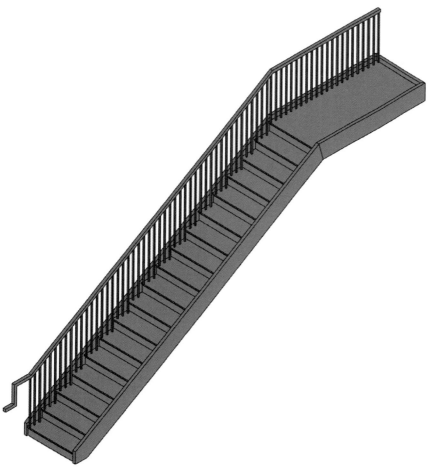

FIGURE 4.27 Completed railing

Designing Ramps

Now that you're familiar with designing a number of stair configurations, ramps should come easily since they are based on the Stair by Sketch tool. It's the same basic process of sketching a desired shape and then completing the sketch, with one major difference: far more frequent landings and a shallower slope.

You access the Ramp tool on the Circulation panel on the Architecture tab. Keep in mind that ramps have different constraints than stairs based on slope and length. Understand that the maximum length of a ramp in one section is 30′-0″ (9000 mm) with a 1:12 slope (8 percent). These parameters can be changed, but by default they correlate to common code requirements.

In the following exercise you will create a straight run ramp between Level 1 and Level 2. Because you're traversing Level 1 to Level 2 (and they are 10′ [3000 mm] apart), this will require a ramp length of 120′ (36,600 mm) at a maximum 1:12 slope, not including landings.

Exercise 4.8: Create a Ramp and Edit the Boundary

To begin, go to the book's web page at www.sybex.com/go/revit2015essentials, download the files for Chapter 4, and open the file c04-ex-4.8start.rvt.

1. Open the example file to the Level 1 view.

2. Select the Architecture tab, and choose the Ramp tool from the Circulation panel.

3. In the Properties palette set the Ramp Type to Ramp 1; the Base Level is Level 1 and the Top Level is Level 2.

4. Using the Run Draw tool, add straight runs similar to Figure 4.28.

5. To get all the landings and ramps into the right location, select the boundary and riser lines after creation and move them using the Move tool on the Modify panel.

   The ramp should look similar to the image in Figure 4.28.

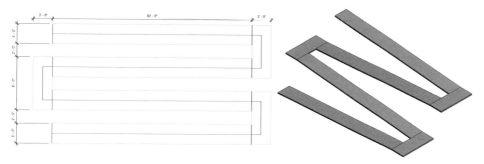

FIGURE 4.28 Straight runs of ramps

6. Click Railing on the Tools panel, and specify the Handrail - Rectangular railing. Click OK to close the dialog.

7. Click Finish Edit Mode to complete the sketch. Open the default 3D view; you should see a similar ramp to Figure 4.29.

The Multistory Top Level parameter is also available for ramps, similar to stairs.

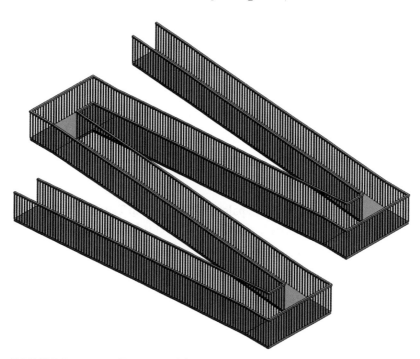

FIGURE 4.29 Ramp runs with associated railings

8. Return to the Level 1 view, select the ramp, and click Edit Sketch.

9. Delete the three green boundary lines that represent the outside edges of the landings, as shown in Figure 4.30.

FIGURE 4.30 The modified ramp in plan with removed exterior boundary edges

10. Select the Boundary tool on the Draw palette, and then choose the Tangent End Arc tool on the Draw panel.

11. Create the new boundaries shown in Figure 4.31 by picking one boundary edge and then the other.

FIGURE 4.31 Modified ramp with curved boundary

12. Click Edit Type to open the ramp type properties.

13. Under Other, set Shape to Solid. Click OK to close the dialog.
    This will create a solid slab ramp instead of maintaining a consistent thickness value.

14. Click Finish Edit Mode to complete the sketch.
    Revit Architecture has already modified the railings to accommodate the new boundary (Figure 4.32).

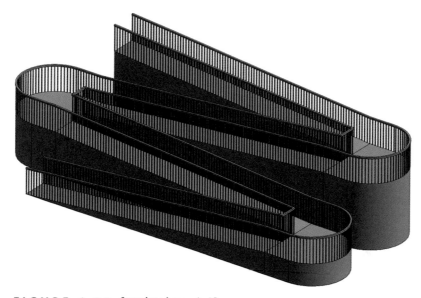

FIGURE 4.32 Completed ramp in 3D

The end exercise file has both ramp shapes, included as two separate ramps, for reference.

Now You Know

Stairs, railings, and ramps are separate object types in Revit Architecture that share some underlying parameters. In addition, objects such as railings do not require a stair to exist; they can be created independently or created using a stair as a host for additional complexity.

In this chapter, you learned about the properties that make up railings and balusters. You created railings and hosted them to stairs. You also customized the top railing and overrode the slope for some railing segments. For stairs you created railings using both the Stair by Component and Stair by Sketch tools. You customized the boundaries and landings and set some to span multiple stories. And finally you created ramps, edited the boundary, and adjusted various properties.

CHAPTER 5

Adding Families

What is a family in the Autodesk® Revit® Architecture software? In the simplest terms, a family can be thought of as repeatable geometry for use in a project. You will now take a step back from the modeling exercises in the previous chapters to develop a better understanding of the basic building blocks that make up a Revit Architecture project.

In this chapter, you'll learn to:

▶ **View and modify the family category**

▶ **Work with and load system families**

▶ **Work with and load component families**

▶ **Work with hosted families**

▶ **Work with face-based families**

▶ **Create an in-place family**

▶ **Find and load family content into your project**

Understanding the Model Hierarchy

In Chapters 2 ("Walls and Curtain Walls"), 3 ("Floors, Roofs, and Ceilings"), and 4 ("Stairs, Ramps, and Railings"), you learned about some basic model elements such as walls, floors, and roofs. These types of objects are known as *system families* in the Revit Architecture software. To better explain what a family is and how it relates to your workflow, let's explore how data is organized in the Revit Architecture platform.

One of the unique characteristics of the program is its inherent model hierarchy. In a simple description, this hierarchy can be expressed as (from broad to specific) *project, category, family, type,* and *instance.*

Project   This is the overall container for the model geometry and information.

5. In the Visibility/Graphic Overrides dialog box on the Model Categories tab, find the Doors category, and place a check in the Halftone column.

6. While still in the Visibility/Graphic Overrides dialog, Model Categories tab, uncheck Visibility for the Furniture category. This will turn off the display of all furniture category elements in this view only.

7. Click OK to close the dialog box. Doors are now displayed in the Level 1 floor plan as halftone, and furniture is no longer visible.

8. Select several of the Level 1 view doors, right-click, and select Override Graphics In View ➤ By Element.

9. Uncheck the box for Visible, and click OK to close the dialog box.
   The door instances are no longer visible in the Level 1 floor plan, yet other door instances are still visible in this and other views (Figure 5.2).

> Use Reveal Hidden Elements to view the doors and set Visible again if needed.

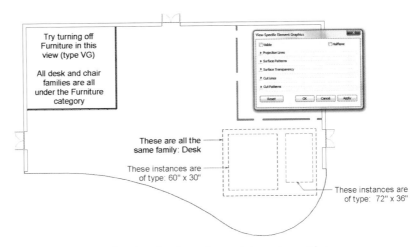

FIGURE 5.2 Completed project, view, and element overrides

In the preceding exercise, you made changes to objects on three levels. Object Styles is a project-wide change for the selected category. The Visibility/Graphic Overrides dialog is a view-specific override for the selected category. Override Graphics In View ➤ By Element is a view-specific override for an instance of the selected category.

Revit Architecture uses three types of families: *system, component,* and *in-place* families. System and in-place families exist only in the project file, whereas component families are created and stored as RFA files outside the project environment. In-place families should be used only for unique, one-of-a-kind objects for which you require nearby geometry as a reference to design.

We will start by exploring system families because they reside directly in the project. Then we will further explore component and in-place families later in this chapter.

Working with System Families

The first type of family you need to understand is the *system* family. The best way to characterize system families is to consider them the *hosts* for other types of geometry. 3D elements such as walls, floors, ceilings, and roofs allow other elements such as doors and windows to exist on them or in them. Other 3D elements, such as stairs and railings, are also system families.

System families are unique in that they create geometry by using a set of rules applied to guiding geometry. If you think about a simple wall, for example, its thickness is defined by a series of structural layers (framing, sheathing, and finishes), its length is expressed by a linear path, and its height is established by some set of horizontal boundaries (either a datum or another element like a roof). As another example, a floor's thickness is defined by a series of structural layers, its vertical location is determined by a datum (level), and its boundary extents are defined by a series of lines. In the project, these rules are the instance and type properties.

Some system families are 2D. These types of system families include text, dimensions, and filled regions. Although the 2D variety of families are still considered system families, we think they are better referred to as *project settings* to avoid confusing them with the more common understanding of families.

Loading System Families

Because system families exist only in the project environment, there are only a few ways you can load them between projects. The first method is to use the Transfer Project Standards command. This method transfers all the families and types in a selected category between projects.

A more informal method of transferring system families is to use the Windows Clipboard functions and copy/paste content between projects. This method is useful if you want to load a limited number of specific families into your active project.

Although it isn't an active loading method, the final technique to manage system families is to include them in your project templates. After you establish a

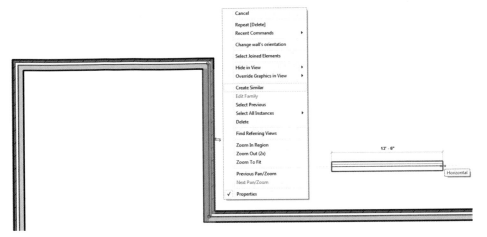

FIGURE 5.4 Using Create Similar to place walls

Working with Component Families

The second type of family you need to understand is the *component* family. These types of families live outside the project environment in RFA files and consist of everything from doors and windows to furniture and equipment. You might think of component families as anything that would be manufactured away from the job site and delivered for installation. This is in contrast to the aforementioned system families, which can be thought of as anything that is assembled at the job site.

Similar to system families, there are also 2D view–specific versions of component families including tags, symbols, detail components, and profiles:

Tags   These component families are scale-dependent annotations that contain what are known as *labels* (the equivalent of block attributes in Autodesk® AutoCAD® software). Labels are special text elements that report information from model elements. Remember, the information (number, name, keynote, and so on) is stored in the component—not in the tag. Tags are attached to system or component families in the project.

Symbols (Generic Annotations)   These component families are scale-dependent annotations that can also contain labels (similar to a tag). The main differentiator between symbols and tags is that symbols can be placed freely and do not need a host in the project. Symbols can also be loaded and used in other families such as tags.

Detail Components   Used in drafting views or to embellish model views, detail components can be used as a more intelligent alternative to simple drafting lines. These components can be tagged or keynoted as if they were model components. You will find much more information on detailing in Chapter 11, "Details and Annotations."

Profiles   Profile families consist of a simple outline of a shape. They are used only in conjunction with other system families such as railings, wall sweeps, and curtain-wall mullions. After you create a profile family, it must be loaded into a project and then associated with a respective system family. A profile's function must be defined in the family parameters (Figure 5.5).

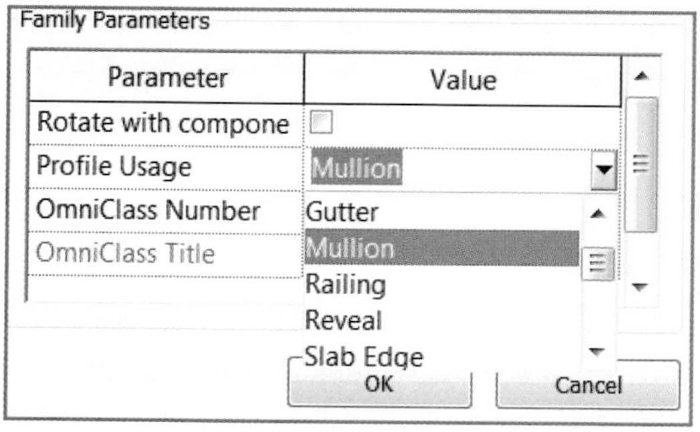

FIGURE 5.5   Defining a profile's function

In the following exercise you will examine the family's category. Then you will explore various methods to load families into your project.

Exercise 5.4: Create a New Family and Load It into a Project

A family's initial category is determined by the template used when the family is created. For this exercise you will be creating a new family using one of the default templates, so no exercise file is required.

1. From the Application button, click New ➤ Family. The New Family – Select Template File dialog box opens (Figure 5.6).
   The list of family templates is consistent with the list of categories you saw in the project environment (Object Styles, Visibility/Graphic Overrides). Each of the available family templates is preconfigured for a specific category in terms of properties, basic materials, and reference planes.

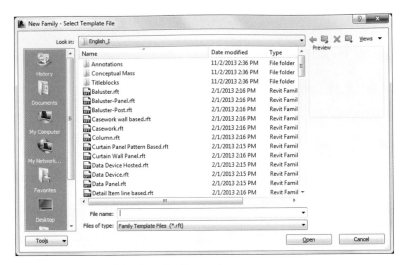

FIGURE 5.6   Selecting a family template

You can change the category of a family in the Family Category and Parameters dialog before loading it into a project; however, frequent manipulation is not recommended because graphics and parameters vary greatly across family categories.

▶

2. Select `Plumbing Fixture.rft` (`Metric Plumbing Fixture.rft`), and click Open.

   The Revit Architecture user interface changes slightly to what is known as the Family Editor (keep in mind that you are still within the main Revit Architecture application).

3. Go to the Create tab's Properties panel, and click the Family Category and Parameters button.

   The Family Category and Parameters dialog box opens (Figure 5.7); it shows the category to which the family is assigned (Plumbing Fixtures).

4. Click OK to close the dialog.

   Next, you want to practice saving this family and loading it into a project (let's pretend for now that you added geometry in the Plumbing Fixtures family.

5. From the Application button, click Save As ➤ Family. Call the family **Plumbing Test** (notice that the file extension is now `.rfa`).

   When the save completes, you'll load this family into a new project.

Load into
Project

Family Editor

6. Create a new project with the default template. Then navigate back to the `Plumbing Test` family. From any tab in the ribbon click Load Into Project.

   If you have more than one project file open, Revit will prompt you for which one to load. If you have one project open, Revit will switch you to the project and immediately start placing the family you just loaded. Notice how Place Component is now active and the `Plumbing Test` family is current.

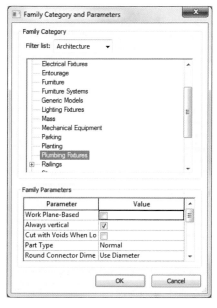

FIGURE 5.7 Viewing the family category and parameters

7. Press the Esc key to cancel placing the family.
   Another method to load families is to use the Load Family tool located on the Insert tab's Load From Library panel.

8. Click the Load Family tool to open the Load Family dialog box, which should open to the family library location.

9. Open the `Doors` folder. Notice that you can select multiple families to load at the same time by holding down the Shift or Ctrl key.

10. Select several families and click Open (Figure 5.8).

> Another method to load families is by dragging and dropping them from any folder on your computer into the Revit Architecture window. This works much the same way as in steps 8–10.

Load Family

Employing Hosted Families

For 3D component families, one key distinction you should understand is whether a family is *hosted*. How do you know whether a family is hosted or unhosted? A simple way to find out is to observe the cursor when a component command is activated and you attempt to place a family. For a hosted family, the cursor will change 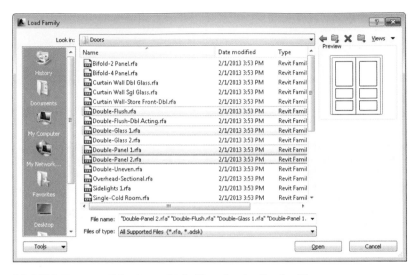 to indicate that you cannot place the family unless you are clicking over a suitable host.

FIGURE 5.8 Selecting multiple files when loading families

The main limitation to a hosted element is that it cannot exist without its host. Certain component families, such as doors and windows, must be hosted because their behavior dictates that they cut their host geometry when placed. For example, you can see this when creating a new door or window family. Notice when opening the family that there is also a system family wall, which serves as the host. Other components, such as furniture, plumbing, and light fixtures, may not need to be modeled as hosted components. These types of objects are placed in a model and almost always maintain a reference to the level on which they were placed.

A slightly different version of a hosted family is known as a *face-based family*. These types of families can be placed on virtually any surface or work plane, but they don't suffer the same limitations as hosted families. Face-based families can exist without a host element even after a host is deleted. When the family is initially created, the family template used will determine the category of the family and whether it is hosted, not hosted, or face-based.

In the following exercise you will work with hosted and unhosted families to explore the default behaviors. In the second exercise you will place and modify face-based families, which are another type of hosted family.

Exercise 5.5: Work with Hosted Families

To begin, go to the book's web page at www.sybex.com/go/ revit2015essentials, download the files for Chapter 5, and open the file c05-ex-5.5start.rvt. The example file should open to the Level 1 view.

1. On the Architecture tab, select the Place A Component tool, and then click Load Family on the ribbon. Navigate to the location of the downloaded exercise family files, and load the ex-5.5hosted.rfa file.

2. In the room at the upper right in the layout, place five instances of the ex-5.5hosted.rfa family on the horizontal partition wall (Figure 5.9). Space the first and last fixtures roughly 3'-0" off the wall ends, and set the other three equally spaced. Notice that you can place these components only on a wall.

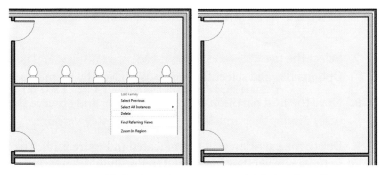

FIGURE 5.9 Placing hosted components and deleting the wall

3. Click the Modify button on the ribbon or press the Esc key to exit the command, and then move the host partition wall up and down. Observe how the components move with the wall.

4. Delete the partition wall where you placed the components in step 2. The hosted plumbing fixtures are automatically deleted when the wall segment is deleted (indicated in Figure 5.9). Use the Undo command to restore the wall and hosted fixtures.

5. Next, you will use the unhosted version of the family. Start the Place A Component command again, and click the Load Family button. Navigate to the c05-ex-5.5unhosted.rfa file, and load it into your project.

3. Before placing a family instance, take note of the ribbon options for Placement.

4. Place on Face and Place on Work Plane are available since this is a face-based family (the default should be Place on Face).

5. With the placement method set to Place on Work Plane, add several instances of the family to the roof and walls. Notice as you move the cursor over an object that the face will pre-highlight, indicating what the face-based family will be hosted to.

6. Now select one of the families you added to a wall.

   In the Properties palette take note of the Host parameter, which is grayed out. This indicates the object the face-based family is attached to. It is an easy reference to know what the family will move with.

7. Now delete one of the project walls the c05-ex-6.Facebased family is hosted to.

   Take note of two things. First, the face-based family is not deleted with the host. And second, the Host parameter has updated to <not associated> to indicate the family is no longer associated with a host (Figure 5.13).

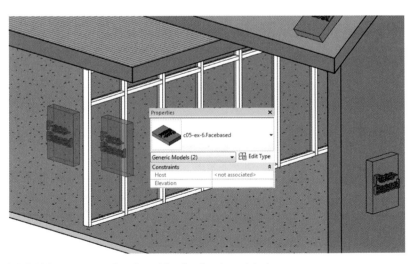

FIGURE 5.13 Face-based family after host deletion

Working with In-Place Component Families

In-Place component families are a special type of component family unique to the current project. They are created in the project environment vs. the Family Editor, so project geometry can be used as a reference. They do not exist outside of the current project. The command is located on the Architecture tab's Component drop-down; it's called Model In-Place.

The major difference between in-place component families and component families is in regard to multiple instances. When component families have multiple instances in the project, updating the family geometry will update all instances. In-Place component families do not support multiple instances of the same family. For this reason, they should be used only for unique geometry since a copy of an in-place component has no relationship to the original (and will not update with changes to the original instance).

In the following exercise you will modify an existing in-place family.

Exercise 5.7: Modify an In-Place Family

To begin, go to the book's web page at www.sybex.com/go/revit2015essentials, download the files for Chapter 5, and open the file c05-ex-5.7start.rvt.

1. Open the project to the default 3D view.

2. Select the countertop extrusion, and choose Edit In-Place on the ribbon to edit the Casework family (Figure 5.14).

FIGURE 5.14 Edit Casework in-place family

Unlike the Family Editor environment, take note that you are editing the family in the context of the project. This can be a very useful technique for custom project families where existing conditions or geometry is required to create the family.

3. Select the counter extrusion and click Edit Extrusion on the ribbon.
   You want to make a slight change to the shape of the countertop to remove the curved edge.

4. Select the curved sketch line and press the Delete key.

5. Add a new sketch line creating a 90-degree corner instead, making sure to close the sketch loop.

6. When the sketch is complete and closed, click the Finish Edit Mode button.
   Notice that you are still editing the family. This is useful if you needed to create additional extrusions or further modify the family.

7. To return to the project and finish editing the in-place family, click Finish Model on the In-Place Editor ribbon panel (Figure 5.15).

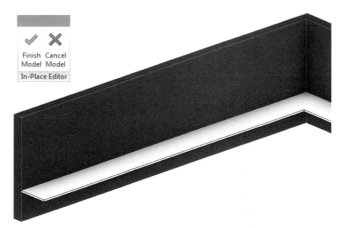

FIGURE 5.15 Complete in-place family

Finding Content

Now that we have reviewed the fundamentals of Revit Architecture families, we'll discuss one of the most important issues you may face as you start designing: the discovery of suitable content. The best place to begin is with the content installed with Revit Architecture. These default families are created with relatively simple geometry and should be sufficient as a basis for the most common building types. If you installed Revit Architecture with the default settings, you will be able to access the default library whenever you use the Insert tab ➤ Load Family command.

Autodesk has created an online resource called Autodesk Seek to provide content for its design software (http://seek.autodesk.com). You can search for families on Autodesk Seek directly from Revit Architecture. Let's explore this option:

1. Go to the Insert tab's Autodesk Seek panel.

2. In the search bar, type **chairs**, and press the Enter key.

3. Your default web browser opens to the Autodesk Seek website.
   The results displayed match the search criteria of *chairs* and are filtered to show only content that offers Revit Architecture families (Figure 5.16).

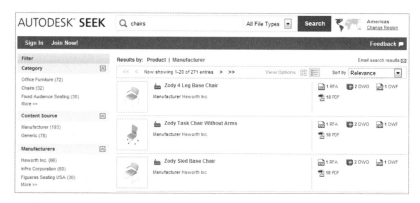

FIGURE 5.16 Content search results in Autodesk Seek

You will note on Autodesk Seek that you can choose from generic or manufacturers' content. The generic content is similar to that found in the installed library. Other content should be used with a level of care. Although an exhaustive review of such criteria is outside the scope of this book, here are some aspects you should understand about component families:

Avoid Imported Geometry   Component families should not be created by simply opening an RFA file and importing 3D geometry from other modeling software. Content with imported geometry may also adversely affect functions such as rendering. For example, a light-fixture family using an imported CAD model might not have the correct material transparency to allow a light source to render properly.

Watch for Over-Modeling   Families should contain only the geometry necessary to document the component. That said, this level of modeling will be slightly different depending on whether you want to create a photorealistic rendering or a construction document. Excessive modeling such as fasteners, switches, knobs, dials, and so on should be avoided.

Use Appropriate Repetition   A Revit Architecture family should have a moderate level of repetition built into it. The repetition should not be too complex (all possible variations in one family) or too simple (a separate family for each variation). Reasonable content will offer a family for each set of common geometry (for example, one model line of a light fixture) with types for subtle variations (the various lamping and size options of that light fixture model).

Now You Know

Families in Revit make up the majority of your project geometry, and we have just scratched the surface in terms of this potential. In this chapter, you've learned about the three categories of families: system, component, and in-place families. You have exercised model hierarchy for Object Styles, view visibility, and element overrides. And you have utilized different categories and options for component families. We will expand on this family knowledge in the next chapter.

CHAPTER 6

Modifying Families

Now that you have added a number of families to your project and the design has progressed, you'll often find it necessary to modify the families. Sometimes swapping out a generic family component for one that is more specific is the best solution. In other cases, it's simply a matter of opening the component family that you started with and tweaking the geometry to better fit your design. Either solution is viable—which you choose depends on the result that is better for your design process.

In this chapter, you'll learn to:

▶ **Modify family categories**

▶ **Edit component families**

▶ **Edit profile families**

▶ **Place and modify detail components**

▶ **Edit a title block family**

▶ **Edit other hosted component families**

▶ **Explore various family tips and best practices**

Modifying 3D Families

As you learned in Chapter 5, "Adding Families," finding and placing content is pretty straightforward, but learning to modify it will take a bit more time. One of the first things you want to consider when loading a family into your project is the level of detail the family displays at different orientations and scales. It's not likely that every part of a component family needs to display at all scales. It's more likely that too much detail will be confusing (particularly at smaller scales). Just a decade or so ago, when we used pencils, knowing when to stop drawing detail was pretty easy. But high-resolution

5. To adjust the settings for displaying information at different scales, navigate to the Manage tab under Additional Settings ➤ Detail Level, as shown in Figure 6.4. Click OK to close the dialog when complete.

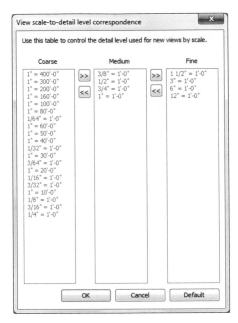

FIGURE 6.4 View Scale-To-Detail Level Correspondence settings

DETAIL LEVEL

In the Detail Level settings, you can choose which view scales use one of three detail levels: Coarse, Medium, or Fine. Based on the scale of the view when a view is first created, some elements will automatically display or hide. But to take advantage of this power, you must make sure the content in your project has the appropriate view scale-to-detail level correspondence. You should also know that the Detail Level and View Scale parameters are separate properties of project views. Thus, if you change the scale of a view, the detail level does not automatically change. The settings shown in Figure 6.4 are automatically applied only when a view is first created.

Let's look at another example of how the detail level controls the visibility of families:

6. Open the elevation view named Cabinet. This view displays a cabinet family with the other objects hidden in the view.

7. The detail level of the view is currently set to Coarse. Change the detail level from Coarse to Medium and notice what happens. You now see the cabinet panels and swing lines in the view (Figure 6.5).

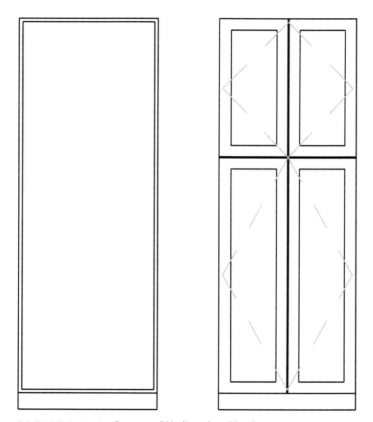

FIGURE 6.5 Coarse and Medium detail levels

8. Change the detail level from Medium to Fine and note what happens again. You now see the cabinet hardware that was not visible in Coarse or Medium detail (Figure 6.6).

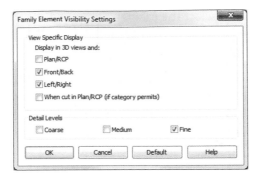

FIGURE 6.8 Set Detail Levels to Fine only

4. Select both cabinet face panel extrusions (there are two separate extrusions that make up the front of the cabinet: the border and the recessed panel). Change the visibility settings so they show up at the Medium *and* Fine levels of detail but not Coarse.

5. Next, you want to do the same for the model lines since they also display in 3D views. An easy way to select only the model lines is to use the Filter tool. Select everything in the 3D view and click Filter from the Selection ribbon panel.

6. Click Check None, and then check Lines (Casework). Click OK to return to the model with only the lines selected (Figure 6.9).

7. Click the Visibility Settings button on the Modify tab of the ribbon and uncheck Coarse. Click OK to return to the model. Next, you want to select just the lines around the hardware extrusions. From the same 3D view window, select around the hardware and use the Filter tool again to select just Lines (Casework). Open the Family Element Visibility Settings dialog again and also uncheck Medium so only Fine is checked (Figure 6.10).

8. Open the Front Elevation view. Select the dashed elevation swing lines (eight of them) and click Visibility Settings from the ribbon. Uncheck Coarse so you also do not see these lines in the project when the cabinet doors are not visible.

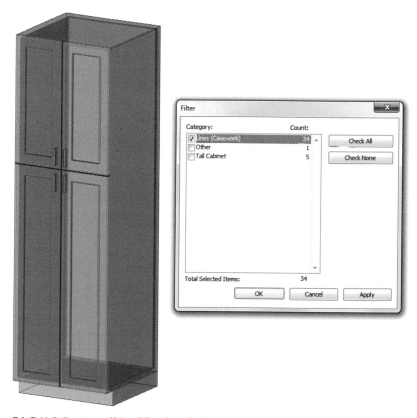

FIGURE 6.9 Using Filter for selection

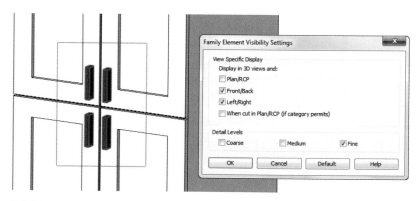

FIGURE 6.10 Window selection and filter

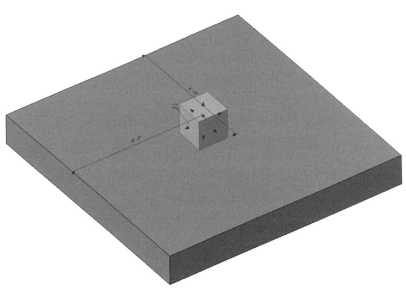

FIGURE 6.12 Editing the face-based family

Keep in mind that changing to or from the Mass category is not allowed.

2. Go to the Create tab's Properties panel, and click Family Category and Parameters.

3. When the Family Category and Parameters dialog box appears, the current category is selected. Select Specialty Equipment from the list (Figure 6.13), and click OK.

In a CAD environment, this step would be just like reloading a block—you're simply updating the element with the new information.

4. Click Load into Project from the Modify tab on the ribbon to reload the family into the project environment.

5. Select the option to override the existing version.
   The family doesn't appear to have changed, but it now schedules according to its new category.

Face-Based_Box

Specialty Equipment (1)

6. To confirm the updated category move your cursor over the family, and the tooltip should display the updated family category.

Alternatively you can select the family and take note of the Properties palette—it will display the family category under the Type Selector.

In the following exercise you will update the origin of a family for both plan and elevation. Then you will load the updated family back into the project.

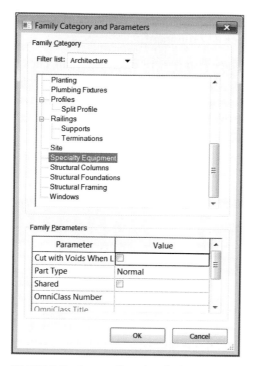

FIGURE 6.13 Changing the family category

Exercise 6.4: Update a Family Insertion Point

To begin, go to the book's web page at www.sybex.com/go/revit2015essentials, download the files for Chapter 6, and open the file c06-ex-6.4start.rvt.

UNDERSTANDING THE INSERTION POINT

The insertion point of a family is important for three main reasons.

▶ A family will flex around its insertion point; therefore, the insertion point is maintained when the family's dimensions change.

▶ If you need to replace one family with another of the same category, they should swap at the same insertion point. Otherwise, if you have a family with an insertion point that is at a corner and swap it with another family whose insertion point is at the center, all the instances of that family throughout your project will shift.

▶ If you need to adjust the default elevation when placing some types of families (such as wall-based families), you can change the reference elevation.

The Defines Origin parameter can also be set in elevation for specific types of families, such as wall-based families. For example, this may be useful for wall cabinets where specifying an exact elevation for the top of cabinets is required.

7. Select the Upper Cabinet family above the desk family, and click Edit Family in the ribbon to open the cabinets in the Family Editor.

8. Open the Placement Side elevation view, and select the reference plane at the top of the cabinets. Select the check box for the Defines Origin parameter in the Properties palette as you did for the reference planes earlier (Figure 6.17). Note that the reference plane elevation is 6'-0" (2000 mm) above the floor line.

Only one horizontal reference plane can be checked in an elevation view for the Defines Origin parameter.

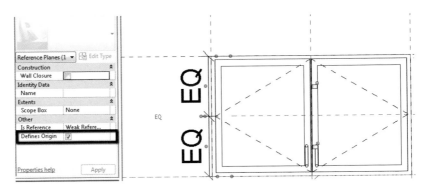

FIGURE 6.17 Reference Planes Defines Origin parameter

9. Click Load Into Project from the ribbon to reload the family into the project, and select Overwrite The Existing Version as you did earlier. Notice that as with the desk, the Upper Cabinet family updates to reflect the new origin.

10. From the Level 1 floor plan view, place a new instance of the overhead cabinet family on any of the walls.

Notice that the default elevation when placing an instance in the floor plan view matches the 6'-0" (2000 mm) elevation of the reference plane. If you select the family, there is an Elevation instance parameter in the Properties palette, which should be set to 6'-0" (2000 mm) (Figure 6.18).

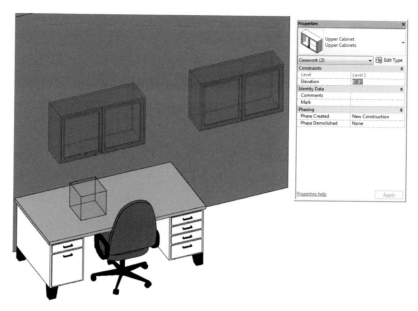

FIGURE 6.18 Elevation parameter available in project

Changing this value will move the cabinet family in elevation relative to the reference plane you set in the Placement Side elevation view. In this example, you can enter a precise value for the top of the cabinets (Figure 6.18).

In the following exercise you will make various changes to a generic host window that is part of the default library. A hosted family has a required relationship to a specific host category, such as Floors, Walls, Roofs, or Ceilings. Without the host, the hosted family can't be placed.

Exercise 6.5: Modify Hosted Components

To begin, go to the book's web page at www.sybex.com/go/revit2015essentials, download the files for Chapter 6, and open the file c06-ex-6.5start.rvt.

1. From the Project Browser under Families, locate and expand the Windows category. Right-click Fixed (M_Fixed), and select Edit from the context menu to open the family in the Family Editor (Figure 6.19).

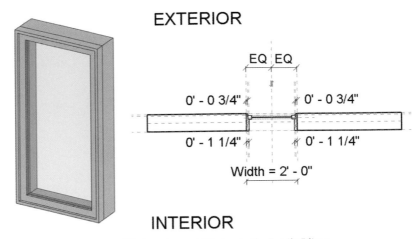

FIGURE 6.19 Window plan and 3D view in the Family Editor

2. You want to keep the existing type, so begin by renaming the family via Save As.

3. Press VV on the keyboard to access Visibility/Graphic Overrides (the left image in Figure 6.20). Make sure the Walls category is checked as shown and click OK. The 3D view now resembles the image on the right in Figure 6.20. Use Zoom To Fit to adjust your view.

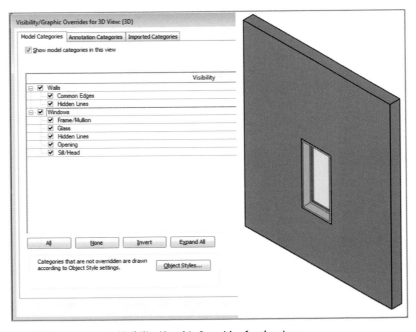

FIGURE 6.20 Visibility/Graphic Overrides for the view

4. Activate the Exterior elevation view from the Project Browser window by double-clicking the Exterior elevation view (Figure 6.21).

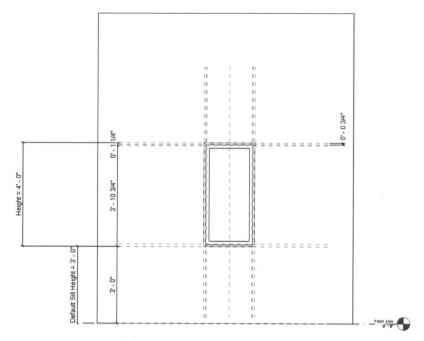

FIGURE 6.21   Reference planes and dimension parameters

Reference planes (displayed as green dashed lines) serve as guides that allow the geometry to flex. As you can see, the window geometry has not been directly assigned to dimension parameters. Instead, the parameters are associated to the reference planes. The window geometry is then associated to the planes. This is the preferred method for constructing family geometry.

5. Go to the Create tab's Datum panel, and click the Reference Plane tool. Draw a horizontal plane around the midpoint of the window.

6. Go to the Modify | Place Reference Plane tab's Measure panel, and click the Aligned Dimension tool. Create a continuous dimension between the two outermost horizontal reference planes and the new plane you created in step 4. Click the temporary EQ icon that is active when you select the dimension just created to establish an equality constraint (Figure 6.22).

No matter how the window height changes, the new reference plane will remain centered.

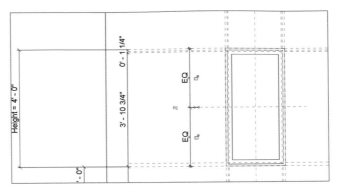

FIGURE 6.22 Adding a new reference plane and keeping it equally spaced

MODIFYING CONTENT IN A FAMILY

Making changes to a hosted component is an important part of modifying existing content. This window family is full of dimension parameters that control different types. You do not need to create new geometry from scratch; you can modify what is already in the family. This approach may seem like cheating, but this is usually how content is modified. In addition to this process being efficient, the geometry that you modify will likely continue to "remember" existing relationships to reference planes and other parameters.

7. Select the Frame/Mullion Extrusion, and click Edit Extrusion from the ribbon (Figure 6.23).

8. Sketch new internal lines, as shown in Figure 6.24, to split the window into three panels. Before you finish the sketch, delete the sketch segments between the new lines (for example, by using the Split tool with the Delete Inner Segment option checked from the Options Bar). When complete, the sketch should look like the blue highlighted area in Figure 6.24.

9. Click the green check button on the ribbon to finish the sketch.

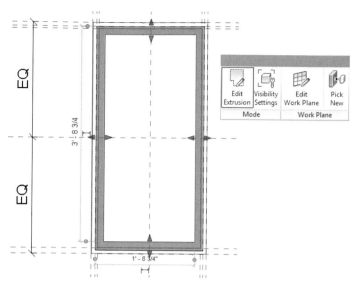

FIGURE 6.23 Frame/Mullion Extrusion

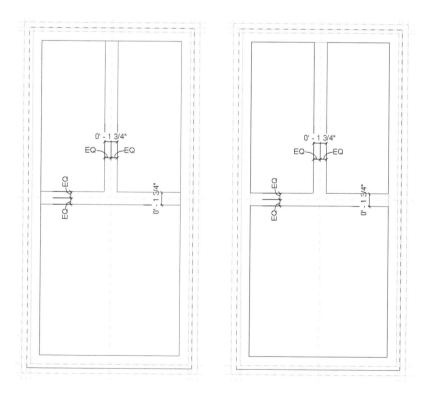

FIGURE 6.24 Edit the existing window frame.

1. From the Project Browser under Families, expand Annotation Symbols.

2. Find the Furniture Tag (M_ Furniture Tag) family, right-click it, and then select Edit from the context menu.

3. In the Family Editor, click the Create tab, and activate the Line tool.

4. Choose one of the arc draw tools and add lines to both sides of the tag.

5. Delete the vertical lines, leaving just the horizontal lines and new arc lines (Figure 6.27). Adjust the horizontal lines if needed.

FIGURE 6.27 New furniture tag shape

6. Click Load Into Project from the ribbon to reload the tag into the project and overwrite the existing tag.

    Notice that the tag instance has updated, and the finished tag should look similar to Figure 6.28. Any tags of the same type in the project will also update to reflect the changes.

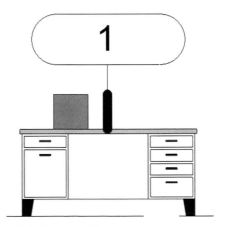

FIGURE 6.28 Completed furniture tag

In the following exercise you will edit and make changes to a profile family, which you will use to generate geometry for the railing.

Exercise 6.7: Edit a Profile Family

To begin, go to the book's web page at www.sybex.com/go/revit2015essentials, download the files for Chapter 6, and open the file c06-ex-6.7start.rvt.

1. In the Project Browser under Families, click to expand Profiles, and then right-click Rectangular Handrail (M_ Rectangular Handrail). Choose Edit from the context menu; Rectangular Handrail (M_ Rectangular Handrail) opens in the Family Editor.

2. Because you want to keep your existing handrail profile intact, from the Application button choose Save As ➤ Family, and name the new profile L Shaped Handrail (M_L Shaped Handrail).

3. There are some parameters that you want to maintain in this family. To make them visible, go to the Visibility/Graphic Overrides dialog box (type VV on your keyboard), and select the Annotation Categories tab. Select all the options, as shown in Figure 6.29, and click OK to close the dialog box.

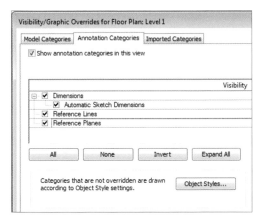

FIGURE 6.29 Adjusting the Visibility/ Graphic Overrides properties of the view

8. Click OK twice to return to the project. The new profile has been associated to the duplicate railing. All you need to do is swap out the default stair railing for the new one! Select the handrails assigned to the stair, and then choose L Shaped Handrail from the Type Selector in the Properties palette (Figure 6.33).

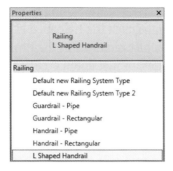

F I G U R E 6 . 3 3 Selecting the new railing

In the following exercise you will edit and make changes to an existing break line family that needs to be updated for your project.

Exercise 6.8: Update Detail Components

To begin, go to the book's web page at www.sybex.com/go/revit2015essentials, download the files for Chapter 6, and open the file c06-ex-6.8start.rvt. The example file should open to the starting view Callout of Section 1.

1. In this detail callout view there is a Break Line family that you need to modify. Select the break line, and click Edit Family from the ribbon to open the family in the Family Editor.

2. Select the break line in the Family Editor, and then click Edit Boundary from the ribbon.

    This element is not a line (see Figure 6.34). It's actually a masking region (kind of like a white solid hatch) that is used to obscure geometry in your project. Some of the boundary line styles are Medium Lines, and some are Invisible Lines.

3. Before you begin to modify the masking region, you should be aware of any constraints established in the family. Press VV on the keyboard. Switch to the Annotation Categories tab, and check both the Dimensions and Reference Planes options. Click OK to close the dialog box.

Text added directly inside a detail component (or standard component family) does not display in the project.

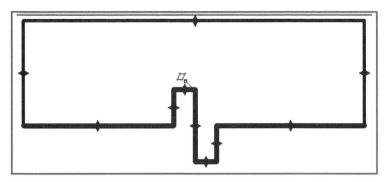

FIGURE 6.34 Selecting and editing the break line

4. In the View Control Bar, change the scale of the view to 1 1/2″ = 1′-0″ (1:10) so the dimensions are more legible. Use Zoom To Fit to see the extents of the constraints (Figure 6.35).

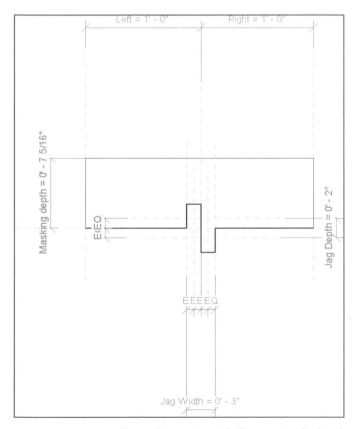

FIGURE 6.35 The masking region with all constraints displayed

5. Delete the squared jag lines, as shown in Figure 6.36.

Notice that the original boundary of the masking region remains displayed in the background for reference.

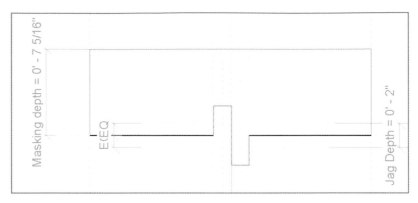

FIGURE 6.36 Delete the existing jag lines in the masking region.

6. From the Create tab in the ribbon, click the Line tool, and make sure Subcategory is set to Medium Lines at the right end of the ribbon. Draw new jag lines, as shown in Figure 6.37. Make sure the lines you draw snap to the midpoints of the previous jag lines and the end points of the remaining straight lines.

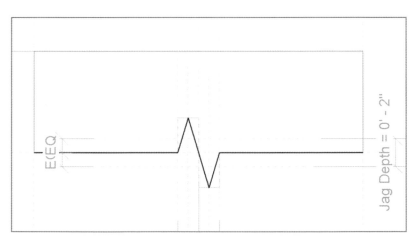

FIGURE 6.37 Sketch new jag lines in the masking region boundary.

7. Click the green check button in the Mode panel of the ribbon to finish the sketch.

8. Go to the Modify | Detail Items tab's Properties panel, and click the Family Types button. Change the Jag Depth value to 0′-6″ (**150** mm), as shown in Figure 6.38, and then click Apply. The size of the jag in the masking region should change. Try a few different values for Jag Depth to make sure the masking region flexes correctly. Click OK to close the dialog box.

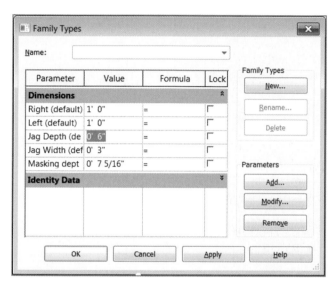

FIGURE 6.38 Change the Jag Depth value to flex the masking region.

9. Click Load Into Project from the ribbon to reload the break line into your project and overwrite when prompted. Your break line will be updated in the Section Callout view to reflect the new shape.

Repeating Details

Repeating details are based on detail component families that are given rules to repeat, based on a defined spacing and rotation. As an example, elements such as brick or concrete masonry units (CMU) in a wall section are elements that repeat on a regular interval. Rather than use an array each time you need to draw these elements in a detail, the repeating detail component allows you to create persistent rules for these components. You can then draw a repeating detail with the ease of drawing a simple line.

Repeating details are located on the Annotate tab's Component drop-down; click Repeating Detail Component. If you edit the type of any existing repeating

It is important to flex families with parametric dimensions before you load them into projects.

detail component, you can create a new type using Duplicate. Then you can set the detail component you want to repeat (any that is loaded into the current project) along with the layout, spacing, and detail rotation (Figure 6.39).

Detail   Specify the detail component to repeat.

Layout   Specify the spacing type to use (such as Fixed Distance or Maximum Spacing).

Inside   Restrict spacing to the path length.

Spacing   Set the distance to space detail components.

Detail Rotation   Apply detail component rotation (None, 90 Degrees Clockwise, 90 Degrees Counterclockwise, and 180 Degrees).

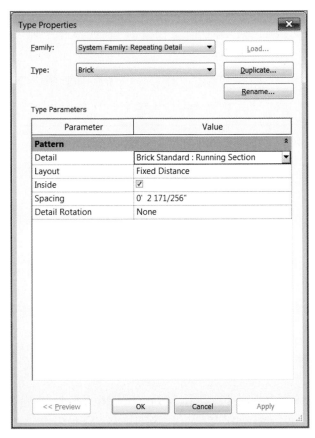

FIGURE 6.39 Repeating Detail Component type properties

In the following exercise you will investigate editing other 2D annotations by modifying the default title block family. Title blocks are considered 2D families, similar to tags and detail components.

Exercise 6.9: Modify the Title Blocks

To begin, go to the book's web page at www.sybex.com/go/ revit2015essentials, download the files for Chapter 6, and open the file c06-ex-6.9start.rvt.

1. Open sheet A101 from the Project Browser. Select the title block, and then choose Edit Family from the ribbon.

2. You need to create a new line type for use in a grid. Go to the Manage tab's Settings panel, and click Object Styles. When the Object Styles dialog box opens, click New under Modify Subcategories. Use the New Subcategory dialog box to create a new line called **Grid Lines**, as shown in Figure 6.40. From the Subcategory Of drop-down, select Title Blocks. Then click OK.

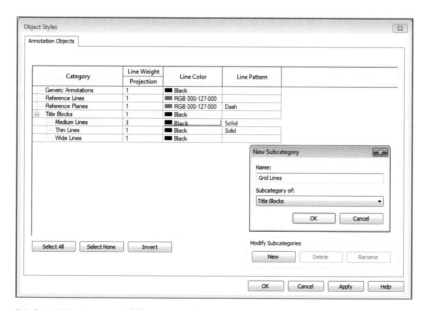

FIGURE 6.40 Adding a new subcategory

3. Select the Line Color option, and modify the color to a light blue. Click OK twice to exit the Object Styles dialog box.

4. You're ready to draw the grid lines. Go to the Create tab's Detail panel, and click the Line tool. Select the Grid Lines subcategory at the right end of the ribbon.

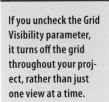

If you uncheck the Grid Visibility parameter, it turns off the grid throughout your project, rather than just one view at a time.

11. Deselect the parameter. When you click OK, the grid is no longer visible in the title block.

Family Tips and Best Practices

The following are some additional tips and best practices for modifying and working with families:

Name Your Reference Planes   After adding new reference planes, make sure to assign them a name in the Properties palette's Name field. This makes it much easier to keep track of each reference plane and allows them to be selected by name when you are editing the work plane.

Edit Work Planes   When working in the Family Editor, you may at times need to move a work plane–based element (such as an extrusion) from one work plane to another. When selecting the element, the option to Edit Work Plane becomes available on the ribbon. You can select from a list of levels and reference planes to move the element to. This is another reason to name reference planes; if Name is blank, it will not appear under the Specify A New Work Plan ➤ Name list.

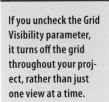

It is much easier to troubleshoot a potential issue before adding additional geometry into the family.

Flex Reference Planes before Adding Geometry   When creating new geometry in a family or adding a parameter to existing reference planes, be sure to properly flex the family before adding geometry. Think of reference planes as the framework for the geometry. First add reference planes, and then add dimensions between the reference planes as needed. Once the dimensions/parameters are in place, the values should be adjusted to ensure the reference planes adjust properly.

Use the Wall Closure Option   For wall-hosted families (such as door and windows), reference planes can be used to determine the point where the wall layers will wrap around the family insert. You can see the difference in Figure 6.44 with Wall Closure checked and unchecked.

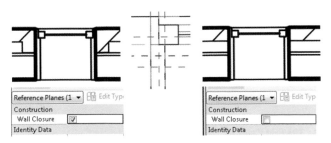

FIGURE 6.44   Wall Closure options

Deal with Filled Regions Blocking Lines in the Title Block This is a common scenario when adding filled regions and lines in a title block family.

1. In the Family Editor, the filled region is added first, and the lines are added second (so the display order appears as expected with the lines on top).

2. Load the title block into the project, and the filled region now overstrikes the lines. One workaround is to start a new Revit generic annotation family and cut and paste the filled regions into the generic family.

3. Lastly, load the generic annotation family into the title block family and locate as needed.

Know When Objects in a Family Cannot Be Deleted Notice that when you start a new family using a default template, some of the existing elements cannot be deleted (such as some reference planes). Why is this? Any geometry that is included as part of the family template cannot be deleted when a new family is created.

◄

While the display order may appear incorrect in the title block family, it should display (and print) correctly in the project.

Create a New Family Template By default, you cannot save an existing Revit family (.rfa) as a family template (.rft). However, you can copy the file in Windows Explorer and rename the extension from .rfa to .rft. Revit will consider this a family template afterward.

Use a "Super" Masking Region By default, masking regions mask model geometry in the project environment, but they do not mask annotation elements such as text, dimensions, tags, or detail lines. If you want to mask model and annotation elements, create a generic annotation family, and add a masking region in the family. When loaded into the project, the generic annotation family will mask both types of objects.

Use a Family Parameter Lock For parameters in a family (Family Types dialog), there is a column with an option to lock. If you lock a parameter in the family, any labeled dimension with that parameter applied will be locked. This means you will be unable to change the value in-canvas. This also means you won't be able to dynamically flex the family in-canvas (such as dragging a reference plane with a labeled dimension attached). This is good to keep in mind if you run into odd behavior when flexing the family; make sure to first confirm whether the parameter is locked.

Importing a 2D Image

To create a 2D digital sketch, Autodesk released a tool for Apple's iPad called SketchBook Pro, which allows you to sketch directly on a tablet using a stylus or your finger like you would use a pen or pencil. The sketch in Figure 7.1 was created on an iPad, but the following steps apply to any scanned image—from either a magazine or trace paper.

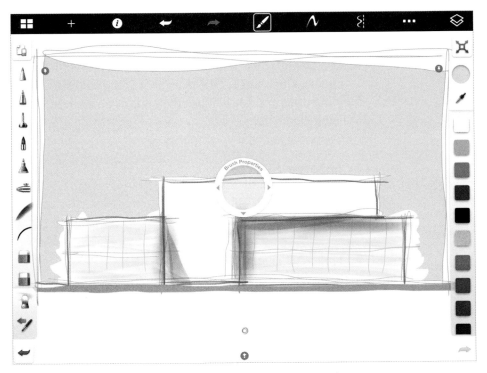

FIGURE 7.1 A 2D sketch from Autodesk SketchBook Pro for iPad

Exercise 7.1: Import and Scale a 2D Image

To begin, go to the book's web page at www.sybex.com/go/revit2015essentials, and download the files for Chapter 7.

1. On the home screen, select Architecture Template to open one of the default Revit Architecture templates. Open the East elevation by double-clicking East in the Project Browser.

2. On the Insert tab, find the Import panel, and click the Image button. Select the `Massing_Sketch.png` file from the `Chapter07` folder. Click the Open button.

3. You may need to zoom out to see the preview graphic consisting of blue grips and an *X*. This preview indicates the size of the image. Click the mouse to place the image. Use the arrow keys to nudge the image so that the ground plane of the building sketch roughly aligns with Level 1, as shown in Figure 7.2.

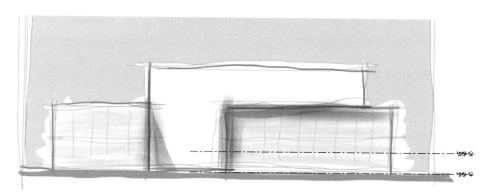

FIGURE 7 . 2 The imported image. Note the location of the levels relative to the ground plane in the image.

4. Zoom into the Level symbols. Select the level line for Level 2. From the Properties palette change the Elevation parameter from 10′-0″ (3.04 m) to **15′-0″ (4.57 m)**; this height is more consistent with commercial construction.

5. The image is a bit out of scale for the Revit model. Select the image and choose the Scale tool from the Modify panel. Refer to Figure 7.3 for the eventual goal.

6. Hover the mouse over Level 1 until it highlights blue and then click. This is the shared base point.

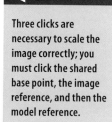

Three clicks are necessary to scale the image correctly; you must click the shared base point, the image reference, and then the model reference.

7. Move your mouse straight up so the cursor roughly aligns with the second floor of the sketch; then click. This is the image reference point.

8. Finally, move you mouse straight down so the cursor aligns with Level 2 of the model; then click. This is the model reference point. After this last click, the image scales to look similar to Figure 7.3.

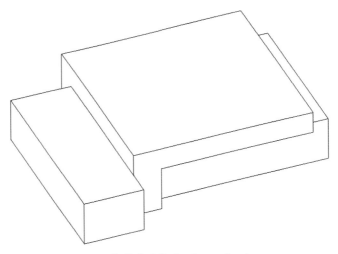

FIGURE 7.5 The linked 3D sketch as an in-place mass

This concludes Exercise 7.2. You can compare your results with the sample file c07-ex-07.2end.rvt available in the download from the Sybex website.

VISIBILITY OF MASS ELEMENTS

The visibility of the Mass element can be tricky. The Massing & Site tab of the ribbon has a drop-down menu with two important options we need to clarify. The first option, Show Mass By View Settings, depends on the Mass category in the Visibility/Graphic Overrides dialog. This means you can enable visibility of the mass per view. The second option, Show Mass Form And Floors, enables you to see the mass in all views but only per session—the visibility of the mass is not saved. This option means the mass probably won't be visible the next time you open the file.

Exercise 7.3: Add a New Level

To begin this exercise, open the file c07-ex-07.3start.rvt.

1. Open the North elevation view from the Project Browser. The mass is visible because the category is checked in the Visibility/Graphic Overrides dialog.

2. Go to the Architecture tab of the ribbon, find the Datum panel, and click the Level tool.

3. In the Draw panel, choose the green Pick Lines tool.

4. On the Options Bar, set the offset value to 15′-0″ (4.57 m).

5. Hover your mouse over the Level 2 annotation element. Look for a dashed blue line to appear *above* Level 2. This dashed line indicates where the new level will be placed; see Figure 7.6.

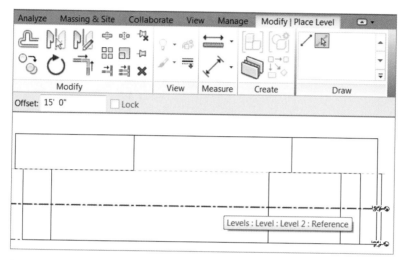

FIGURE 7.6 Use the Pick Lines tool to create a new level.

6. Click to place the new level, called Level 3, at 30′-0″.

This concludes Exercise 7.3. You can compare your results with the sample file c07-ex-07.3end.rvt from the download for this chapter.

LEVELS VS. REFERENCE LEVELS

If you copy a level instead of create a new one, Revit creates a *reference level*. Reference levels are useful for Top Of Parapet or Bottom Of Eave—architectural references that don't need a floor plan. Reference levels show black level symbols in elevation views instead of blue level symbols. The blue symbols are hyperlinked to their corresponding floor plan. Try double-clicking the blue level marker, and Revit will open the floor plan view.

Exercise 7.4: Calculate Mass Floor Area

Open the file c07-ex-07.4start.rvt from the download to start this exercise.

1. The file should open in the 3D view. Select the Mass element, and click the Mass Floors button in the ribbon.

2. Check the box next to Levels 1, 2, and 3; then click OK. The Mass element has been divided at the level intersections.

3. Click the View tab; then click the Schedules button and choose Schedule/Quantities.

▶

Schedules are covered in more depth in Chapter 12, "Drawing Sets."

4. In the New Schedule dialog, review the list of categories on the left, find Mass, and expand it. Click Mass Floor, and click OK.

5. In the Schedule Properties dialog, in the Fields tab, choose the following parameters from the list on the left; then click the Add button. Add them in this order: Mass: Family, Level, Floor Area (see Figure 7.7).

FIGURE 7.7   The list of Mass Floor parameters

6. Click the Formatting tab. Choose the Floor Area parameter from the list on the left. Check the Calculate Totals box from the options to the right.

7. Now click the Sorting/Grouping tab. Check the box for Grand Totals; then choose Totals Only from the drop-down list. Click OK.

8. You can see that the Floor Area total is roughly 51,500 SF (15,697.2 m), as shown in Figure 7.8. This is valuable information to have early on in schematic design.

This concludes Exercise 7.4. You can compare your results with the sample file c07-ex-07.4end.rvt that you downloaded earlier.

<Mass Floor Schedule>		
A	B	C
Mass: Family	Level	Floor Area
Trapelo Sketch	Level 1	18590 SF
Trapelo Sketch	Level 2	18590 SF
Trapelo Sketch	Level 3	14340 SF
		51521 SF

FIGURE 7.8 The Floor Area schedule

Exercise 7.5: Reload a Linked Sketch

To begin, open the file c07-ex-07.5start.rvt.

1. If the design changes, the 3D sketch changes, and you'll need to update the linked building mass by reloading the .sat file. Open the 3D view.

2. Go to the Insert tab of the ribbon, and click the Manage Links button on the Links panel. Click the CAD Formats tab of the dialog.

Manage
Links

3. Click the cell named Trapelo_Sketch.sat. Then click the Reload From button from the options below it.

4. The Find Link dialog appears. From the Chapter 7 folder, choose the file named Trapelo_Sketch_Update.sat and click Open.

5. Click OK to confirm the changes in the Manage Links dialog.

6. The building mass has updated slightly. Revit automatically recalculates the mass floors as well. Go to the Schedules/Quantities node of the Project Browser and open the Mass Floor Schedule. The Floor Area total is now 55,201 SF (16,825 m).

This concludes Exercise 7.5. You can compare your results with the sample file c07-ex-07.5end.rvt available in the download.

IMPORT CAD VS. LINK CAD

If you plan to iterate on the building form and building area using FormIt and Revit, you should link your .sat file instead of importing it. This will allow you to reload the link easily when changes are made.

Creating Revit Elements from a Mass

Once your mass is approximately the right size and shape, you can start to advance from the conceptual design phase to early design development. The mass itself has few properties aside from area and volume. You need to add building elements like floors, walls, and curtain systems to enclose and define your building. Revit uses the mass as an armature to place these real model elements upon.

Exercise 7.6: Create Floors from a Mass

To start this exercise, open the file c07-ex-07.6start.rvt.

1. The file should open in the 3D view. Go to the Massing & Site tab, find the Model By Face panel, and then click the Floor tool.

2. Select the three mass floors; this is easy to do because you are allowed to select only mass floors in this tool.

3. After choosing all three mass floors, click the Create Floor button in the ribbon. Now you have real Revit floors that will be displayed in all views. The benefit of creating floors by face is that you don't need to sketch a custom shape for any of your floors—Revit uses your mass floor to automatically generate the floor outline.

This concludes Exercise 7.6. You can compare your results with the sample file c07-ex-07.6end.rvt.

You can change the *type* of floor you want to create before you make floors by face. Choose from the Type Selector drop-down after you start the Floor By Face command but before you click the Create Floor button.

Exercise 7.7: Create Walls from a Mass

Open the file c07-ex-07.7start.rvt to begin this exercise.

1. In order to make the next steps easier, turn on Face Selection. Find the Modify button on the far-left side of the ribbon, and click the Select button underneath it. Now check the box next to Select Elements By Face.

2. Go to the Massing & Site tab, find the Model By Face panel, and then click the Wall tool. You will place solid walls now and place glass walls in the next exercise. Hover your mouse over one of the third-floor walls, as in Figure 7.9. Click to place a new wall.

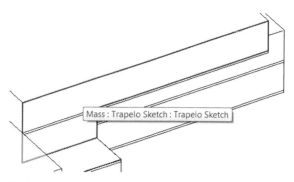

FIGURE 7.9 Place a solid wall by face.

3. It is difficult to differentiate the mass from the Revit wall. To show which walls have been created and which still need to be placed, adjust the graphics by changing the visual style from Hidden Line to Shaded.

4. Open the Visibility/Graphic Overrides dialog by typing the shortcut **VG**. Find the Floors category, and uncheck the box next to it.

5. Also in the Visibility/Graphic Overrides dialog, find the Mass category and click into the cell in the third column titled Transparency; then click again to make the Surfaces dialog appear. Set the Transparency value to **50**. Click OK.

6. Also in the Visibility/Graphic Overrides dialog, expand the Mass node. Uncheck the box next to the Mass Floor subcategory. Click OK to confirm all of these changes to the Visibility/Graphic Overrides dialog. Make sure that the Massing & Site tab has the Show Mass By View Settings button enabled.

7. Now the mass and walls are distinguishable. Click the Massing & Site tab, choose the Wall By Face tool, and click to place walls until the volume in the middle of the mass looks like Figure 7.10.

This concludes Exercise 7.7. You can compare your results with the sample file c07-ex-07.7end.rvt.

This concludes Exercise 7.9. You can compare your results with the sample file c07-ex-07.9end.rvt.

CREATE MASSES DIRECTLY IN REVIT

In the previous exercises you used an imported FormIt model as your mass geometry. That is not the only way to progress from the schematic to the conceptual design. Revit has robust geometry-creation tools within the massing environment, including extrusions, blends, sweeps, swept blends, and revolves. After you've created basic forms, you can use voids to carve away at your initial form.

We don't have the space to go into all of the Revit massing tools. However, modeling more complex masses is something that you'll likely want to learn and experiment with. You may want to investigate the *Mastering Revit Architecture 2015* book from Sybex for insights into these tools.

Now You Know

Masses are an essential part of the early conceptual design process when using Revit. Working with other software tools like Autodesk FormIt or Autodesk Sketchbook Pro is supported and even encouraged to get the design right before moving into design development. The information gleaned from simple massing studies in Revit can inform building orientation and building program validation. The nice part of the Revit massing workflow is that you can add walls and floors to the mass faces, thus allowing your design to maintain its intelligence into the early stages of design development.

CHAPTER 8

Rooms and Color Fill Plans

In the previous chapters of this book, we discussed creating physical elements such as walls, floors, roofs, stairs, and railings; however, one of the most important elements in architecture is the spaces bounded by those physical elements. In the Autodesk® Revit® Architecture software, you have the ability to create and manage rooms as unique elements with extended data properties. Keeping room names and areas coordinated has the potential to free hours of manual effort for more productive and meaningful design-related tasks. Once rooms are tagged, you'll be able to create coordinated color fill plans that automatically reflect any data about the rooms in your project. Any changes to the rooms are immediately reflected throughout the entire project.

In this chapter, you'll learn to:

▶ **Define rooms in spaces**

▶ **Add a room tag**

▶ **Modify a room boundary**

▶ **Delete a room object**

▶ **Generate color fill room plans**

▶ **Modify a color scheme**

▶ **Add tags and color fill to sections**

Defining Rooms in Spaces

Rooms are unique types of objects because they do not have a clear physical representation like other model elements such as furniture and doors. Their horizontal extents are automatically determined by bounding objects in the

Room Separation Lines

Room Separator

There are times when you have a large, central open space, as in the following exercise, and you'll need that space to be subdivided and tagged into smaller functional areas. You don't want to add walls to carve the large space into smaller areas, especially if they don't exist in the program; fortunately, there's a better option. You can draw spatial dividers known as *room separation lines*. Room separation lines are model lines, and they show up in 3D views. The great thing about them is that they allow you to create spaces without using 3D geometry.

Deleting Rooms

While using the Room command, you can place a room and a room tag simultaneously; however, deleting a room completely from a project takes multiple steps. If you simply delete a room tag, the room object remains in the space. You can add another tag to the room object later or tag it in a different view.

If you delete a room object, the definition of the room remains in your project until you either place another room using the same definition or delete it in a room schedule. We'll explore this behavior later with a quick exercise in which you will delete a room object, observe the unplaced room in a schedule, and then replace the room object in the floor plan.

Exercise 8.1: Add Rooms and Room Tags

From the book's web page (www.sybex.com/go/revit2015essentials) download the project file c08-ex8.1start.rvt. Make sure the Level 1 floor plan is activated and set the scale to 1/4" = 1'-0" (1:50).

To add a room to your project, follow these steps:

1. Go to the Architecture tab's Room & Area panel, and select the Room tool.

2. Hover over an enclosed space, and notice that the room boundary highlights, indicating the space in which you're about to place a room object (Figure 8.3).

3. Click to place a room in the upper-left space on the Level 1 floor plan. Notice that the default room tag indicates only the room name and number (Figure 8.4), but more options are available.

You don't have to tag rooms as you place them, but by default this option is selected, as highlighted in the Modify | Place Room tab.

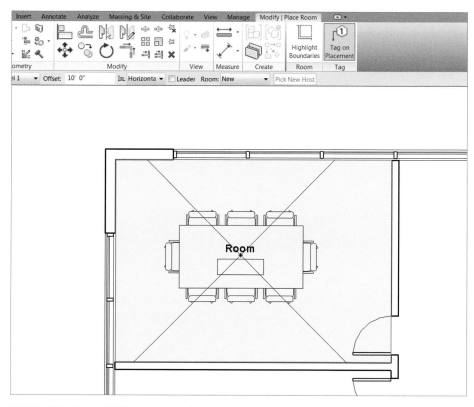

FIGURE 8.3 Adding a room and a room tag

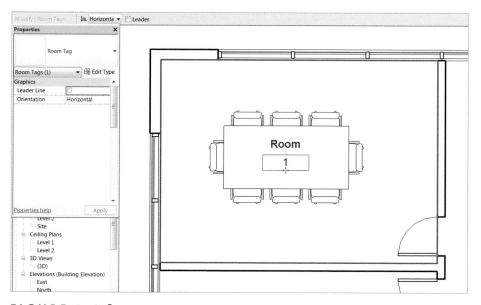

FIGURE 8.4 Room tag

4. Click the Modify button or press the Esc key to exit the Room command, and then select the room tag.

5. Choose the Room Tag With Area option from the Type Selector in the Properties palette. The room tag shows the area based on your project units (Figure 8.5). In this case, the room is 230 square feet (21 square meters).

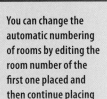

The area feature of the room tag is incredibly helpful, because you can constantly confirm that your spatial program requirements are being maintained as your design develops. As locations of walls are modified, the room object will adjust accordingly and display the recalculated area values.

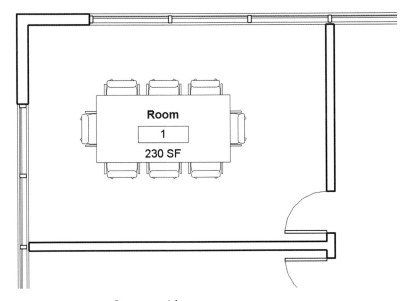

FIGURE 8.5 Room tag with area

You can change the automatic numbering of rooms by editing the room number of the first one placed and then continue placing others.

6. Select the first room you created by finding the set of invisible crossing vectors, and examine its properties in the Properties palette. You can modify the room name and number here by editing the settings under Identity Data or by directly editing the Name and Number values in the room tag. It doesn't matter where you modify the data, because it is all stored in the room object. This makes it easy to create various plan diagrams to suit your needs.

7. Change the name of the room to **Small Meeting**, and change the number to **101**.

8. Place some other rooms within the floor plan, and observe how the numbering scheme has changed.

9. Select the wall at the right edge of the Small Meeting room, as shown in Figure 8.6, and move it 2′-0″ (600 mm) to the left.

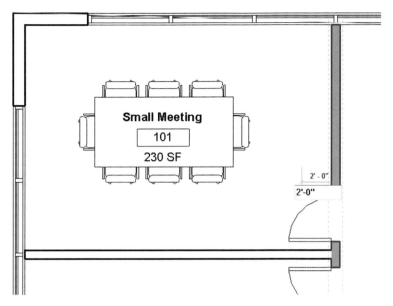

FIGURE 8.6 Moving the wall

Notice that the moment you release the wall, the room updates with the new area information, which is immediately reported by the room tag (Figure 8.7).

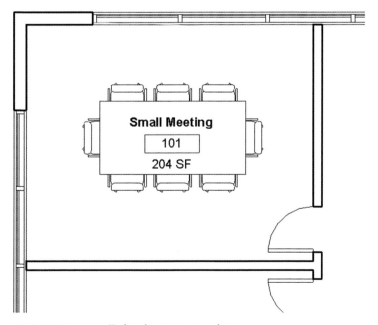

FIGURE 8.7 Updated room space and tag

10. Continue to add rooms and tags to the Level 1 floor plan, as shown in Figure 8.8. The rooms will be numbered as you place them, so place the rooms according to the numeric sequence shown in the figure, starting with room 102.

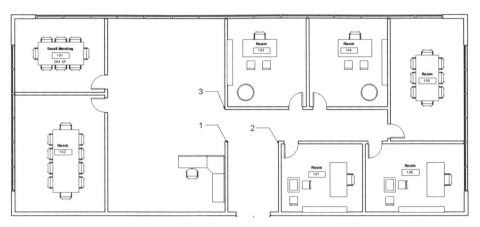

FIGURE 8.8 Adding rooms and tags

You can compare the file in its finished state on the book's web page. Download the file titled c08-ex8.1end.rvt.

Exercise 8.2: Modify a Room Boundary

From the book's web page (www.sybex.com/go/revit2015essentials), download the project file c08-ex8.2start.rvt. Make sure the Level 1 floor plan is activated. If you completed Exercise 8.1, you can begin the following steps where you left off.

Follow these steps to subdivide the open space in the project into three functional spaces:

> You can turn off room separation lines in the Visibility/ Graphic Overrides for a view under the Lines category.

1. Start to add a tag to the large central open space and notice that the space will be tagged as a single room (Figure 8.9). In this exercise you want this space to be divided into smaller functional areas. Do not place a room object in this area.

2. Return to the Room & Area panel on the Architecture tab of the ribbon, and select Room Separator.

3. Draw a line between the wall intersections labeled 1 and 2 in the sample file.

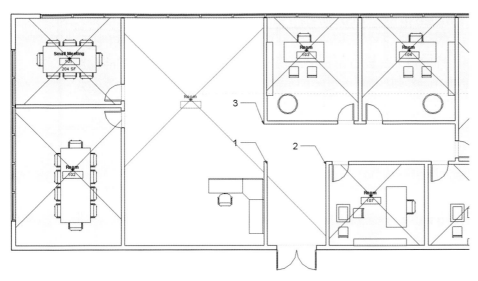

F I G U R E 8 . 9 Tagging a large space

By default, these lines are thin and black, but you can change the settings to make it easier to distinguish the lines from other elements. You will modify the Room Separator line style to be more visible in a working view, but it will be turned off in your sheet views.

4. Go to the Manage tab's Settings panel, click the Additional Settings flyout, and select Line Styles. Maximize lines to view all available line styles in the sample project.

Additional Settings

5. Change the default values for the <Room Separation> lines as follows:

   ▶ Line Weight: 5

   ▶ Color: Blue

   ▶ Line Pattern: Dot 1/32″ (Dot 1 mm)

6. Click OK to finalize these changes.

7. Sketch another room separator in the sample file between the wall intersections labeled 1 and 3.

8. Add rooms and room tags to the subdivided open space, as shown in Figure 8.10.

◀

You may customize these settings for room separation lines, or any other line style, as needed by your project.

**Certification
Objective**

Compare your completed exercise to the example file c08-ex8.3end.rvt, available for download from the book's web page.

Generating Color Fill Room Plans

Creating color fill plans in Revit Architecture is easier to accomplish than most other design applications. Because color fills are associated with the elements of your building design, they will constantly update as existing information is modified or new information is added. This allows you to focus on communicating rather than coordinating your design information — as if resolving your design isn't already hard enough!

In the following exercises, we will explore how to add a color scheme to your floor plan and section and how to modify the values. By default, solid fill colors will be automatically assigned to each unique value in a color scheme. Fortunately, you can completely customize the colors and fill patterns for the scheme.

Exercise 8.4: Add and Modify a Color Scheme

From the book's web page (www.sybex.com/go/revit2015essentials), download the project file c08-ex8.4start.rvt.

1. Go to the Annotate tab's Color Fill panel, and select the Color Fill Legend tool.

2. Click anywhere in the whitespace of the drawing area, and a dialog opens that allows you to select the space type and color scheme (Figure 8.13).

3. Set Space Type to Rooms and Color Scheme to Name. Click OK.

You can create any number of color schemes based on various data in your project model. For example, you could also create color fill legends according to department or custom parameters such as floor finish, occupancy type, and even ranges in area.

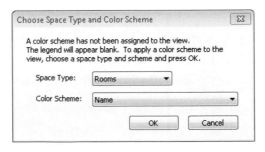

FIGURE 8.13 Defining the color fill legend

4. To edit the color assignments, select the color fill legend in the plan view. You can then select the Edit Scheme tool from the contextual ribbon. You can also access the same settings in the Properties palette for the current view. Just find the Color Scheme property, and click the button in the parameter field.

5. Select the Edit Scheme tool, which opens the Edit Color Scheme dialog where all the values are available for editing (Figure 8.14).

You can edit the color in the Edit Color Scheme dialog as well as the fill pattern. Changing the fill pattern is helpful if you want to create an analytic fill pattern for a black-and-white or grayscale print.

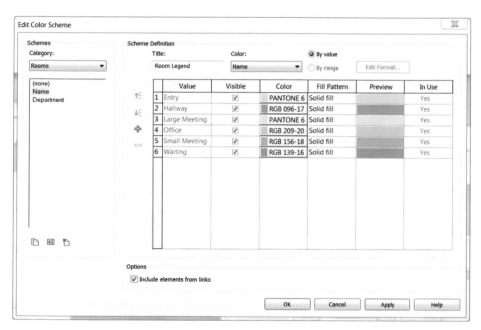

FIGURE 8.14 Edit Color Scheme dialog

6. With the Edit Color Scheme dialog box open, select the Color field in the row for Small Meeting. The Color dialog box opens.

7. Modify the color values to **Red 203**, **Green 242**, and **Blue 222**. When you complete the changes, the fill color automatically updates to reflect your changes (Figure 8.15). Notice that all rooms that share the same name also share the same color fill. Color fills were automatically created based on assigned room names. If a room is renamed, the color fill should change accordingly.

Tag
All

▶

You have two options to tag the room objects. Room Tag lets you place each tag manually. This approach is fine for a small project, but on larger projects you can save time by using the Tag All Not Tagged command to automatically place tags in the current view.

4. Select the Tag All tool on the Annotate tab's Tag panel. Doing so opens the Tag All Not Tagged dialog, allowing you to tag numerous element categories in a view simultaneously. You need to tag only rooms in this exercise, so select the Room Tags category, as shown in Figure 8.19, and then click OK.

FIGURE 8.19 Adding room tags with the Tag All Not Tagged tool

5. To move a tag that may be overlapping element geometry, click the Modify button in the ribbon (or press the Esc key), select a tag, and drag it using the grip that appears near the selected tag (Figure 8.20). You can also grab and drag a tag directly without selecting it first.

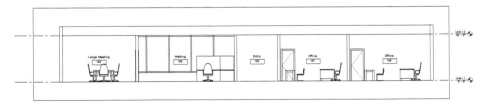

FIGURE 8.20 Room tags shown in section

6. Return to the Annotate tab's Color Fill panel, select the Color Fill Legend tool, and place the legend in the section view.

7. Once again, set Space Type to Rooms and Color Scheme to Name, and click OK. The rooms are filled with the same pattern and color in the section view as the color fill in the plan view, as shown in Figure 8.21.

You can set the color fills in the section view to describe Department or other values, while the room tags display the room name.

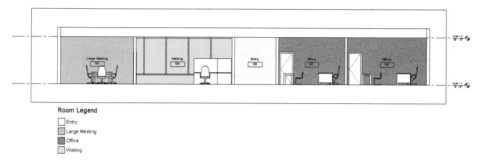

Room Legend

☐ Entry
☐ Large Meeting
■ Office
☐ Waiting

FIGURE 8.21 Room colors in the section view match the plan colors.

8. Notice in Figure 8.21 that the color fill is obscured by some of the model elements such as doors and furniture. This is because the color fill can be placed as a background or foreground in any view. Find the Color Scheme Location parameter in the Properties palette for the settings of the current view. Change this setting to Foreground, and observe how the color fill display is modified.

Compare your completed section to the example file c08-ex8.5end.rvt, available for download from the book's web page.

NOW YOU KNOW

In this chapter you have learned how to define rooms within spaces and add room tags to those spaces. You have also learned how to modify the boundary of a room object based on your project's program and delete a room object if necessary. In addition, you created a color fill plan and section by adding a color scheme to your views and modifying the color values.

There's a lot of wonderful functionality with regard to rooms, room tags, and color fills that we haven't been able to cover in this brief chapter. Instead, we focused on typical uses to get you up to speed so you can be confident and productive as quickly as possible.

discuss how to create materials in your model. Then we'll apply a material to a brick wall.

Exercise 9.1: Define a Material

To begin, go to the book's web page at www.sybex.com/go/revit2015essentials, download the files for Chapter 9, and open the file c09-ex-09.1start.rvt.

Materials

1. Go to the Manage tab of the ribbon and click the Materials button on the far left. This will open the Material Browser, where you define your materials.

2. The Material Browser dialog has a list of material names to the left with a very helpful search box at the top of the list. Type the word **Brick** into the search field, and the list will filter to only one material named Masonry - Brick.

The Graphics tab has a Shading property. These settings are displayed only in views set to Shaded or Consistent Colors.

3. Click the Masonry - Brick material and notice that the properties on the right update, as in Figure 9.1. You're looking at the Graphics tab of the material's properties. You can choose a unique color for the brick by clicking the Color button under the Shading header. You can also redefine the surface pattern. The brick pattern looks good, so leave it as is.

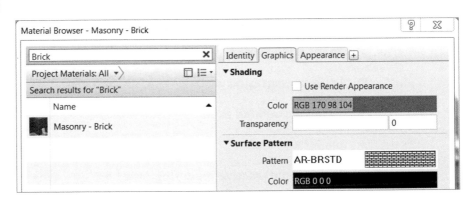

FIGURE 9.1 Search results for Brick and the Graphics tab

4. Now click the Appearance tab and you'll see a small rendered preview of the brick material (Figure 9.2). Below this preview are properties that affect the way this material looks in renderings. Above the preview image are buttons related to the material asset. Click the icon with arrows that allows you to replace the asset with a different material map.

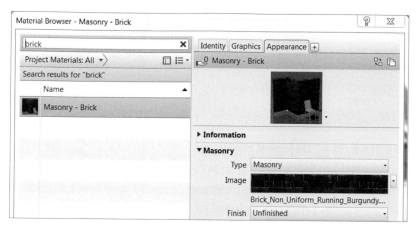

FIGURE 9.2 The Appearance tab and the swap icon

5. The Asset Browser dialog appears (Figure 9.3), and it also has a search field at the top. Type in **Brick**; then click the Masonry option under the `Autodesk Physical Assets` folder and you'll see a variety of options. You should drag the column widths so you can see the material asset names. Double-click the Non-Uniform Running - Red brick material.

The settings specified on the Appearance tab are displayed only in renderings and views set to Realistic visual style.

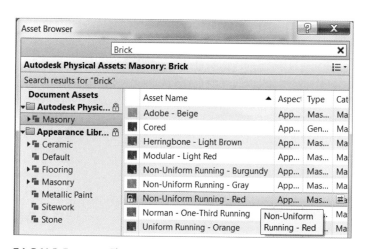

FIGURE 9.3 The Asset Browser

6. The preview in the Appearance tab updates. Click the Graphics tab again, and check the Use Render Appearance box; see Figure 9.4. The shaded color updates to reflect an average color sample from the material render appearance! This is very helpful for consistency between different visual styles. Click OK to exit.

Exercise 9.3: Presentation Elevation View

To begin, open the file `c09-ex-09.3start.rvt`.

1. Find the East elevation in the Project Browser. Right-click the name East and choose Duplicate View, and then in the flyout menu choose Duplicate (Figure 9.6). This will make a copy of the view but without copying detail annotation elements.

FIGURE 9.6 Duplicate a view from the Project Browser.

2. Right-click the newly created view in the Project Browser, named East Copy 1, and click Rename. Type in a new name, **East – Presentation**. Next you'll turn off the level markers and the reference planes in the view.

3. Select one of the green dashed reference planes, right-click, and choose Hide In View ➤ Category (Figure 9.7). All of the reference planes are now hidden. Select one of the level datum graphics, right-click, and choose Hide In View ➤ Category. Notice that all of the level markers are now hidden.

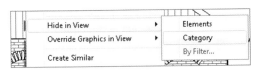

FIGURE 9.7 Hide the category in the view.

Click the Reveal Hidden Elements light bulb on the View Control Bar to see hidden elements and categories. You can select any hidden element and chose Unhide Category from the ribbon. This will make the element visible.

4. Now you are ready to embellish the presentation drawing with effects found in the Graphic Display Options (GDO) dialog box. Open the GDO from the Properties palette by clicking the Edit button next to the Graphic Display Options view parameter.

5. Click the Smooth lines with anti-aliasing check box. This effect improves the line quality in the view dramatically. It has a negative performance impact, so use it in presentation views only.

6. Expand the Shadows section. Click the Cast Shadows and Show Ambient Shadows check boxes. Click the Apply button at the bottom of the dialog to see the effect these have on the model.

7. Expand the Sketchy Lines section, and click the Enable Sketchy Lines check box. Slide the Extensions control to 7, and click Apply.

8. Expand the Lighting option, and find the Shadow slider. Slide this to the left to make your shadows lighter. Click Apply and adjust until you're satisfied with the darkness of the shadows.

9. Expand the Background section, and choose Gradient from the options. Click Apply. You should see something similar to Figure 9.8. Click OK to close the GDO dialog.

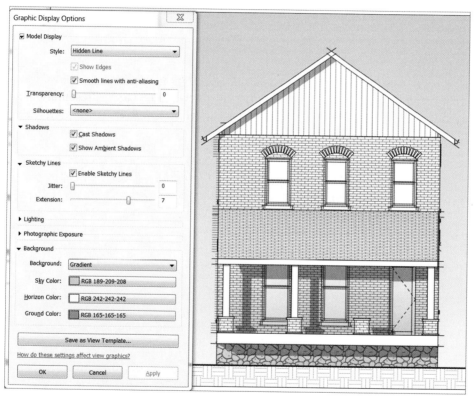

FIGURE 9.8 Elevation presentation view and GDO settings

10. The visual effects are all set, but the crop region needs to be adjusted. Select the crop region. Note the blue grips that appear in the middle of the edges. These can be dragged so that the elevation is framed as you desire.

11. Once you have the elevation centered in the crop region, you can turn off the crop region. The control for the crop region visibility is on the View Control Bar at the bottom of the screen. Click the Hide Crop Region button. Now you have an elevation view ready to be placed on a sheet.

This concludes Exercise 9.3. You can compare your results with the sample file c09-ex-09.3end.rvt available in the download for the chapter.

Exercise 9.4: Presentation 3D View

To begin, open the file c09-ex-09.4start.rvt from the files you downloaded earlier.

1. Open the 3D view titled 3D Isometric in the Project Browser. The view is locked so that you cannot accidentally change the angle of the view. You can unlock the view by clicking the Unlock 3D View button on the View Control Bar, next to the Hide Crop Region button.

2. Click the Visual Style button on the View Control Bar, and choose the Shaded option. Then click the Visual Style button again, but this time click the Graphic Display Options text at the top of the list. This is a handy shortcut to the GDO dialog.

3. Check the Smooth lines with anti-aliasing, Cast Shadows, and Show Ambient Shadows check boxes. Turn on Enable Sketchy Lines and set the Extension slider to 7. Set the Background option to Gradient. Click Apply to see these effects.

4. Expand the Lighting option, and adjust the Shadows, Sun, and Ambient Light slider controls. The Sun and Ambient Light sliders make an impact when your visual style is set to Shaded or Realistic. Set each of these values to 40, and click OK. You may need to zoom in a bit to see the surface patterns; then your view should look like Figure 9.9.

5. Select the large brick wall that is blocking your view into the house. Right-click and choose Override Graphics In View ➤ By Element. Click the arrow next to Surface Transparency, and use the slider to set the value to 40. Click OK, and deselect the wall by hitting the Esc key twice.

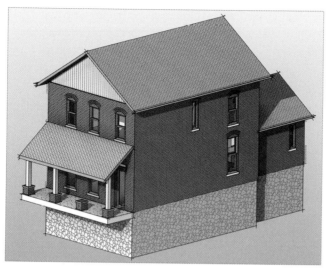

FIGURE 9.9 3D Isometric with GDO effects

6. You can see into the house, but the brick surface pattern is still
    obscuring the view. Select the wall again, right-click, and choose
    Override Graphics In View ➤ By Element. Expand the Surface
    Patterns control, and uncheck the Visible parameter as in Figure 9.10
    Click OK, and then press Esc to deselect the wall.

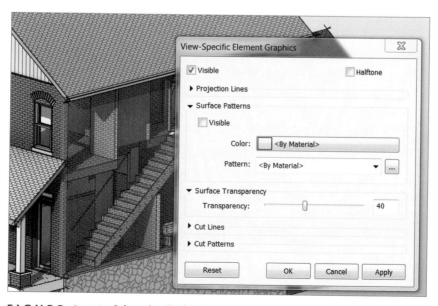

FIGURE 9.10 Selected wall and element overrides

This concludes Exercise 9.4. You can compare your results with the sample file c09-ex-09.4end.rvt available in the chapter's download.

Exercise 9.5: 3D Exploded View

To begin, open the file c09-ex-09.5start.rvt from the files you downloaded for this chapter.

1. Open the view 3D Exploded View. Select the large brick wall, and click the Displace Elements button on the View panel of the Modify tab.

2. A widget appears with green, red, and blue arrows. This widget allows you to move the displaced set of elements. Click and drag the red arrow away from the house. Release the mouse button to place the wall. With the wall still selected, look in the Properties palette for the X Displacement value. Set this value to 25'-0" (7.6 m).

3. Since the windows are hosted in the wall, they move with it. You can displace these elements farther from the wall. Hover your mouse over a window, and click the Tab key until the window highlights. Select the window; then hold down Ctrl and click the other two windows so you have all three selected. Click the Displace Elements button. In the Properties palette, set the X Displacement value for the window to 20'-0" (6 m).

4. Click any of the displaced windows to select the displacement set, and from the ribbon choose the Path tool. Hover your mouse over one of the corners of your displaced windows. Click to add a dashed line back to where the element originated; repeat for the other corners. If you accidentally add a path line you don't want, you can select it and click Delete on the keyboard.

5. Now you can add graphic effects using the GDO to make a beautiful and informative presentation drawing using steps from the previous exercises. Your results may look like Figure 9.11.

This concludes Exercise 9.5. You can compare your results with the sample file c09-ex-09.5end.rvt from the files you downloaded.

Displacing elements is a view-specific override much like hiding an element in one view only. The changes made using Displacement will not affect the model or any other views of the model.

▶

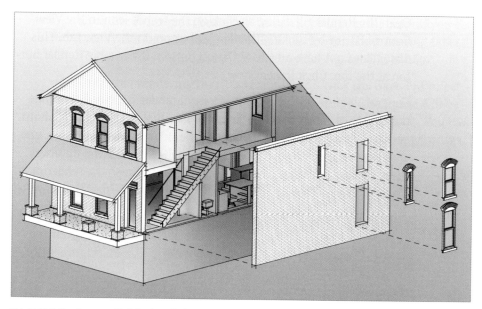

FIGURE 9.11 Finished exploded vie

Rendering

The technique of computer rendering is a complex science that has been simplified and tailored for architects in Revit Architecture. There are many expert computer renderers in the architecture field, and we recommend this tutorial as an initiation to the activity of rendering.

Exercise 9.6: Render a View

To begin, open the file c09-ex-09.6start.rvt from the chapter's download.

1. Open the view 3D Cover Shot. Get a quick preview of the render appearance of the materials used in the scene by switching to the Realistic visual style using the View Control Bar.

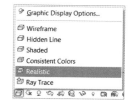

 N O T E   If you're unsatisfied with any of the materials used, you can refer to Exercises 9.1 and 9.2 to change the material's Appearance properties (not the material's Graphics properties) to make the material more suitable for renderings.

Exercise 9.7: Interactive Rendering

To begin, open the file c09-ex-09.7start.rvt from this chapter's download.

1. In the Project Browser, find the 3D Views node, right-click the 3D Cover Shot view, and choose Duplicate View ➤ Duplicate. Rename the new view **Interactive Rendering**.

2. Change the visual style of the new view to Ray Trace using the View Control Bar. Ray Trace is a temporary, interactive rendering mode, where you can use the navigation wheel to pan, zoom, and orbit your model.

3. The rendering in Ray Trace mode will automatically start. At first, the image will be low quality and low resolution, but it will improve quickly the longer you let the view idle. When you begin navigating your model, the rendering will restart as soon as you stop navigating and let the view idle.

4. To change the rendering settings for Ray Trace mode you need to access the GDO. You can type the keyboard shortcut **GD** or click the Visual Style menu on the View Control Bar. Make sure to change the Background setting to Sky. You can also brighten the scene using the Manual option of Photographic Exposure. Finally, you can change the Sun location in Sun Settings; click OK. In the GDO dialog click Apply to preview the changes, and then click OK when you're ready.

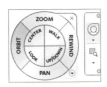

5. Click the navigation wheel icon, and use the Orbit command, the Walk command, as well as the Pan command to move the camera to various vantage points. The Look command is especially useful on interior scenes. When you find an interesting camera angle, you can stop there and let the Ray Trace rendering improve for a few seconds (Figure 9.14).

6. You can save the image to the Renderings node of your Project Browser. Just click the Save button from the ribbon. Name the rendering **Back of House**. Finally, click the Close button on the ribbon to exit Ray Trace mode.

This concludes Exercise 9.7. You can compare your results with the sample file c09-ex-09.7end.rvt from the files you downloaded for this chapter.

FIGURE 9.14 A Ray Trace rendering after 15 seconds

Exercise 9.8: Cloud Rendering

Autodesk offers a very reliable and fast service that will render your Revit views in the cloud, thus allowing you to continue working while your renderings process somewhere else.

To begin, open the file c09-ex-09.8start.rvt in this chapter's download.

1. To use the cloud service, click the Render in Cloud button on the View Tab. You will be asked to sign in using your Autodesk 360 account. Create an account if you don't have one. After logging in, you should see a Render in Cloud dialog box with a few informational steps for cloud rendering; click Continue.

2. The Cloud Rendering Service provides an interface for you to select which views you'd like to have rendered. First, expand the 3D View drop-down; then check the boxes for Interactive Rendering and 3D Cover Shot — or choose to render all five of the 3D views.

3. There are other options below, but as long as you set Render Quality to Standard and Image Size to Medium (1 Mega Pixel), then the renderings do not cost any cloud credits; they are free! See Figure 9.15.

each user in the project by the username specified in the Application menu ➤ Options ➤ General ➤ Username (Figure 10.1). It is critical that each user working in the model have a unique username.

Username

duellr

You are currently not signed in to Autodesk 360. When you sign in, your Autodesk ID will be used as your username.

Sign In to Autodesk 360

FIGURE 10.1 Username setting in Options

In the following exercise you will open an existing project, enable worksharing, and save it as the new Central Model.

Exercise 10.1: Enable Worksharing

Worksets

To begin, go to the book's web page at www.sybex.com/go/revit2015essentials, download the files for Chapter 10, and open the file c10-ex-10.1start.rvt.

1. With the example file now open, navigate to the Collaborate tab and select the Worksets tool. The initial Worksharing dialog box (Figure 10.2) appears, outlining the worksets that project elements will be assigned to.

▶

The first time you click the Worksets tool it enables worksharing. Clicking the tool afterward allows you to access and modify worksets.

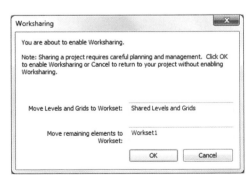

Worksharing

You are about to enable Worksharing.

Note: Sharing a project requires careful planning and management. Click OK to enable Worksharing or Cancel to return to your project without enabling Worksharing.

Move Levels and Grids to Workset: Shared Levels and Grids

Move remaining elements to Workset: Workset1

OK   Cancel

FIGURE 10.2 The initial Worksharing dialog box

2. By default, datum objects are moved to a workset called Shared Levels and Grids. Project content that is not view specific (geometry and rooms) is all assigned to Workset1. Click OK to continue.

THE CENTRAL MODEL

In a real-world project, the next step would be to save your Central Model onto a server location so the entire project team could access the model. Team members never work in the Central Model directly; instead, they create and work in local files. Local files communicate directly with the Central Model, so it needs to be in a location accessible to all.

3. The Worksets dialog box (Figure 10.3) opens next. Your username appears in the Owner field. Currently, you own everything in the project since you enabled worksharing. Click OK to continue.

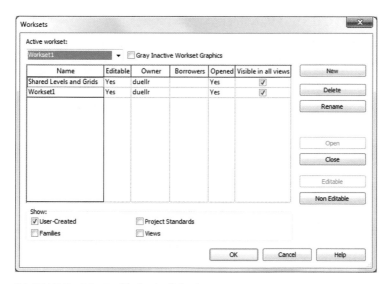

FIGURE 10.3 Worksets dialog box

Before you save the model, think about where you need it to be located. When the Central Model is saved, it will include the file location as part of the project, so it can't be easily moved afterward.

4. Next, you want to save the project as the Central Model. Navigate to Application ➤ Save As ➤ Project. Before clicking Save, click the Options button. In the File Save Options dialog you can confirm that this will be the Central Model. You will have other options, such as the maximum number of backups that Revit Architecture will maintain for the Central Model (Figure 10.4). Confirm that Make this a Central Model after save is checked, and click OK to close the File Save Options dialog.

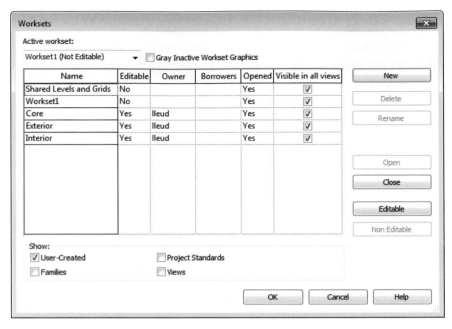

FIGURE 10.7 Creating additional worksets

8. Open the Visibility/Graphic Overrides dialog box for the view (keyboard shortcut **VG**).

   Notice that there is now an additional Worksets tab that didn't exist before worksharing was enabled. This tab allows you to turn off the visibility of elements based on their workset assignment. When you've finished examining this tab, close the local file before starting the next exercise.

WORKSET VISIBILITY

Worksets can be used as an additional method to control the visibility of elements in a view. The default setting for workset visibility is Use Global Setting (Visible) under the view Visibility/Graphic Overrides ➢ Worksets tab. On a view-by-view basis, you can override the Visibility setting should you need to show or hide elements on individual worksets.

In the following exercise you will assign model elements to worksets and adjust the workset visibility settings of the view.

Exercise 10.3: Assign Elements to Worksets and Control Visibility

To begin, make sure that you've downloaded the file c10-ex-10.3start.rvt, but don't open it just yet.

1. From the Revit Application menu click Open, browse to c10-ex-10.3start.rvt, and select the file. Check Detach From Central and click Open. This will allow you to open an existing Central Model to resave it in a new location.

2. When the Detach Model From Central dialog displays, choose Detach And Preserve Worksets. This will preserve all worksets in the model. After the model opens, click the Save button and save as c10-ex-10.3start.rvt. If you're saving the file in the same location as the original model, when prompted that the workset file already exists, click Yes.

3. The model should open the Level 1 floor plan view. Open the Visibility/Graphic Overrides dialog box for the view (keyboard shortcut **VG**) and click the Worksets tab. Change the Visibility setting for the Core, Exterior, and Interior worksets to Hide (Figure 10.8). Click OK to close the dialog.

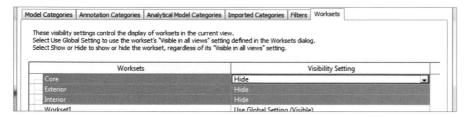

F I G U R E 1 0 . 8 Workset Visibility setting

4. Window-select the elements shown in Figure 10.9. While the elements are selected, click the Filter tool from the Selection contextual panel. Uncheck Room Tags and click OK to close the Filter dialog (Figure 10.9).

Filter

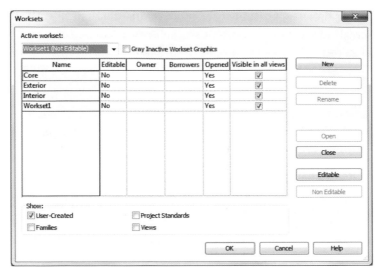

FIGURE 10.14 Relinquished elements and worksets

In the following exercise you will work with closing and opening worksets in an existing model to globally update visibility.

Exercise 10.4: Open and Close Worksets

To begin, make sure you've downloaded the file c10-ex-10.4start.rvt, but don't open it just yet.

OPEN OR CLOSE WORKSETS

In addition to the workset per-view visibility settings, worksets can be opened or closed for the entire project. Doing so will globally turn on or off the visibility of everything on that workset, for all project views regardless of the Workset Visibility setting for that view. This is a great method to improve performance or turn off the display for entire portions of the model.

1. From the Revit Application menu browse to c10-ex-10.4start.rvt and select the file. Check Detach From Central and click Open. This will allow you to open an existing Central Model to resave it in a new location.

2. When the Detach Model From Central dialog displays, choose Detach
   And Preserve Worksets. This will preserve all worksets in the model.
   After the model opens, click the Save button and save as c10-ex-
   10.4start.rvt. If you're saving in the same location as the original
   model, when prompted with The Workset File Already Exists,
   click Yes.

3. Open the Worksets dialog box under Collaborate ➤ Worksets (or
   click the Worksets button on the status bar). Notice that currently
   all worksets are set to Open (the Opened column will read Yes or No
   accordingly).

4. In this example model there are five worksets: Doors-Windows, Exterior
   Walls, Furniture, Interior Walls, and Rooms. Select the Furniture and
   Rooms worksets and click the Close button (Figure 10.15). You can
   select multiple worksets at the same time by holding down the Ctrl key
   while selecting.

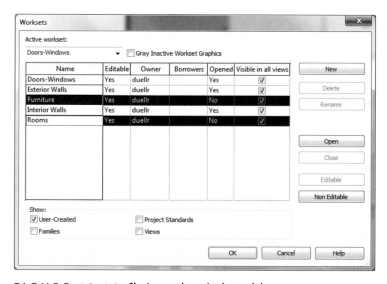

FIGURE 10.15 Closing worksets in the model

5. Click OK to close the Worksets dialog. Notice in the Level 1 view that
   the rooms and furniture are no longer visible. Unlike the Visibility/
   Graphic Overrides Worksets Visibility setting, closing or opening a
   workset will affect all views.

Selecting the Owners display mode will show you exactly which elements belong to which users (Figure 10.20).

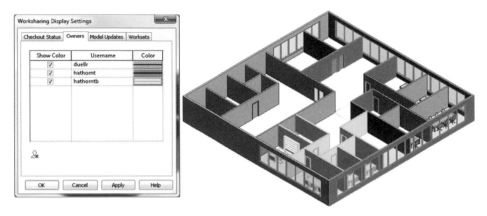

FIGURE 10.20 Owners tab

The Worksets tab helps you visualize elements based on the workset to which they're associated (Figure 10.21).

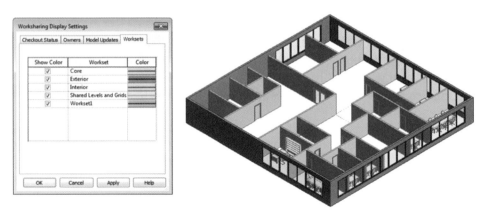

FIGURE 10.21 Worksets tab

Editing Requests

Eventually while working on a project team, another user will own an element you need to modify. For you to modify that element, the other user will first need to relinquish it. Let's take UserA and UserB as a simple example for this scenario:

1. UserA attempts to modify a wall but receives an error dialog noting that UserB currently owns the element (Figure 10.22).

2. UserA clicks the Place Request button in the dialog so UserB will be notified (Figure 10.22).

FIGURE 10.22 Placing a request

3. While UserB is working in their local file, they receive a modal Editing Request Received dialog indicating that UserA has requested the wall element.

4. UserB clicks Grant, which will give editability to UserA for that wall element only (Figure 10.23).

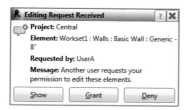

FIGURE 10.23 Granting a request

5. Lastly, UserA receives the confirmation dialog back that UserB has granted permission to edit the wall element (Figure 10.24).

In this example, no further action is required from UserA; UserA can start making modifications to the wall. The editing request serves as both a user notification system and an automated method to swap element ownership.

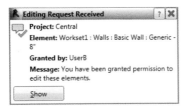

FIGURE 10.24 Granted confirmation

Worksharing Best Practices

Now that you have a general understanding of how worksharing and worksets operate, take a moment to consider a few best practices.

Think of worksets as containers.   Worksets aren't layers as in CAD. Think of them as containers for major systems in your building (interior, exterior, roof, core, and so on). You need to manage or be mindful only of objects that belong to user-created worksets, such as the following:

> ▶ Datum (levels and grids)
>
> ▶ Geometry (building elements that show up in multiple views)
>
> ▶ Rooms (the spaces that can be tagged)

Be mindful of the active workset.   As you're creating datums, geometry, or rooms, be mindful of the active workset. And keep in mind that Revit Architecture automatically manages the worksets for everything else (views, families, and project standards), and these cannot be changed by the user.

Borrow elements on the fly.   Don't check out worksets by making the entire workset editable. Instead, just borrow elements on the fly. This approach lets you avoid many conflicts that occur when one person needs to modify something you own (but don't really need) in the model. With the interconnected nature of buildings, you don't even need to deliberately make an element editable. All you have to do is modify an existing element, and Revit Architecture will transparently borrow it for you. This works the same when adding new elements as well.

Associate linked files to their own workset.   Associate any linked files to their own workset. Then you can open and close the worksets associated to those links. This strategy is much more predictable than loading and unloading links (which will have an effect on everyone working on the project). Opening or clos-ing a workset affects only your local file.

Stay out of the Central Model.　Stay out of the Central Model—don't move it, and don't rename it (unless you know what you're doing). Opening the Central Model restricts access by the files that are trying to connect to it. And if you break something in the Central Model, you'll break the connections that oth-ers have from their local file, which means they may end up losing their work (which in turn means your team will not like you).

Open and close worksets selectively.　Selectively opening and closing worksets is a lot faster than opting to modify the visibility settings of multiple views or using hide/isolate on a view-by-view basis. If you're supposed to be working only on the core and internal areas of a multistory building, opening only the work-sets associated to those areas will save a lot of computing power.

Now You Know

This chapter served as both an introduction and reference to multi-user collaboration in Revit Architecture. You enabled worksharing and saved a Central Model. Next, you created a local file, created and modified worksets, controlled element visibility using those worksets, and explored the options to save your work back to the Central Model. Moving forward, this chapter should also serve as a strong reference for more advanced collaboration topics such as workshar-ing display modes and editing requests. We concluded this chapter with some best practices for you to utilize on your real-world projects.

CHAPTER 11

Details and Annotations

So far, you have used the Autodesk® Revit® Architecture software to create walls, doors, roofs, and floors; to define space; and to bring your architectural ideas into three-dimensional form. In each of these cases, the geometry is typically modeled based on a design intent, meaning that your goal hasn't been to model everything but rather to model enough to demonstrate what the building will look like. To this end, it becomes necessary to embellish parts of the model or specific views with detailed information to help clarify what you've drawn. This embellishment takes the shape of 2D detail elements in Revit Architecture that you will use to augment views and add extra information.

In this chapter, you will learn to:

▶ **Create a detail**

▶ **Enhance a detail with 2D elements**

▶ **Create a repeating detail component**

▶ **Annotate a detail**

▶ **Create a legend**

Creating Details

Even when you're creating details, Revit Architecture provides a variety of parametric tools that allow you to take advantage of working in *building information modeling (BIM)*. You can use these tools to create strictly 2D geometry or to augment details created from 3D plans, sections, or callouts. To become truly efficient at using Revit Architecture to create the drawings necessary to both design and document your project, you must become acquainted with these tools.

These view-based tools are located on the Detail panel of the Annotate tab (Figure 11.1). This small but very potent toolbox is what you will need to familiarize yourself with in order to create a majority of the 2D linework and components that will become the details in your project. To better understand how these tools are used, let's quickly step through some of them. You're going to use the Detail Line, Region, Component, and Detail Group tools, because they will make up your most widely used toolkit for creating 2D details in Revit Architecture.

FIGURE 11.1 The Detail panel of the Annotate tab

Detail Line

The Detail Line tool is the first tool located on the Detail panel of the Annotate tab. This tool is the closest thing you'll find to traditional drafting in the Revit Architecture software. It lets you create view-specific linework using different lineweights and tones, draw different line shapes, and use many of the same manipulation commands you would find in a CAD program, such as offset, copy, move, and so on.

DETAIL LINES ARE VIEW SPECIFIC

Detail Lines appear only in the view in which they're drawn. They also have an arrangement to their placement, meaning you can layer them under or on top of each other or other 2D objects. This feature is especially important when you begin using regions, detail lines, and model content to create details.

Using the Detail Line tool is fairly easy. Selecting the tool changes your ribbon tab to look like Figure 11.2. This tab has several panels that allow you to add and manipulate linework.

FIGURE 11.2 The Detail Line toolset

This tab primarily contains three panels: Modify, Draw, and Line Style. You've seen the Modify panel before. It contains the host of tools you've used so far for walls, doors, and other elements. Here you can copy, offset, move, and perform other tasks. The Draw panel lets you create new content and define shapes, and the Line Style drop-down allows you to choose the line style you'd like to use.

Region

The next tool on the Detail panel of the Annotate tab is the Region tool. *Regions* are areas of any shape or size that you can fill with a pattern. This pattern (much like a hatch in AutoCAD) dynamically resizes with the region boundary. Regions layer just like detail lines do and can be placed on top of, or behind, other 2D linework and components. Regions also have opacity and can be completely opaque (covering what they are placed on) or transparent (letting elements show through).

There are two types of regions: filled regions and masking regions.

Certification Objective

Filled Regions   *Filled regions* allow you to choose from a variety of hatch patterns to fill the region. They are commonly used in details to show things such as rigid insulation, concrete, plywood, and other material types defined by a specific pattern.

Masking Regions   *Masking regions*, on the other hand, come in only one flavor. They are white boxes with or without discernible border lines. Masking regions are typically used to hide, or *mask*, from a view certain content that you don't want shown or printed.

Component

The Component drop-down menu lets you insert a wide array of component types into your model. These are 2D detail components, or collections of detail components in the case of a repeating detail. Detail components are schedulable, taggable, keynotable 2D families that allow an additional level of standardization in your model.

Detail components are 2D families that can be made into parametric content. In other words, a full range of shapes can be available in a single detail component. Because they are families, they can also be stored in your office library and shared easily across projects.

To add a detail component to your drawing, follow these steps:

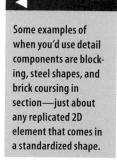

Some examples of when you'd use detail components are blocking, steel shapes, and brick coursing in section—just about any replicated 2D element that comes in a standardized shape.

1. Select Detail Component from the Component drop-down list located on the Annotate tab.

2. Use the Type Selector to choose from detail components that are already inserted into the model.

If you don't see a detail component you want to insert in the Type Selector, try this:

1. Click the Load Family button on the Modify | Place Detail Component tab.

2. Insert one from the default library or your office library.

Arranging Elements in the View

Knowing how to change arrangement is an important part of detailing so you don't have to draw everything in exact sequence. Arrangement allows you to change the position of an element, such as a line or a detail component, relative to another element. Much like layers in Adobe Photoshop or arrangement in Microsoft PowerPoint, Revit Architecture allows you to place some elements visually in front of or behind others. Once an element or group of elements is selected and the Modify menu appears, on the far right you'll see the Arrange panel.

From here, you can choose among four options of arrangement:

► Bring to Front

► Bring Forward

► Send to Back

► Send Backward

Bring Forward and Send Backward are available selections using the drop-down arrows next to Bring to Front and Send to Back, respectively. Using these tools will help you get your layers in the proper order.

Certification Objective

Repeating Detail Component

Repeating elements are common in architectural projects. Masonry, metal decking, and wall studs are some common elements that repeat at a regular interval. The Revit Architecture tool you use to create and manage these types of elements is called the repeating detail component, and it's located in the Component flyout on the Annotate tab.

This tool lets you place a detail component in a linear configuration in which the detail component repeats at a set interval; you draw a line that then becomes your repeating component. The default Revit Architecture repeating detail is common brick repeating in section. Creating elements like this not only lets you later tag and keynote the materials but also allows you some easy flexibility over arraying these elements manually.

Before you create a repeating detail component, let's examine one such component's properties. Select Repeating Detail Component and choose Edit Type from the Properties palette to open the Type Properties dialog box shown in Figure 11.3.

FIGURE 11.3 Type Properties dialog box for a repeating detail

Here's a brief description of what each of these settings does:

Detail   This setting lets you select the detail component to be repeated.

Layout   This option offers four modes:

> **Fixed Distance**   This represents the path drawn between the start and end points when the repeating detail is the length at which your component repeats at a distance of the value set for Spacing.
>
> **Fixed Number**   This mode sets the number of times a component repeats itself in the space between the start and end points (the length of the path).
>
> **Fill Available Space**   Regardless of the value you choose for Spacing, the detail component is repeated on the path using its actual width as the Spacing value.
>
> **Maximum Spacing**   The detail component is repeated using the set spacing, and the number of repeated components is set so that only complete components are drawn. Revit Architecture creates as many copies of the component as will fit on the path.

Inside   This option adjusts the start point and end point of the detail components that make up the repeating detail. Deselecting this option puts only full components between start and end points rather than partial components. As an example, if you have a run of brick, selecting the Inside check box will make a partial brick at the end of the run. If you want to see only full bricks (none that would be cut), deselect the option.

Spacing   This option is active only when Fixed Distance or Maximum Spacing is selected as the method of repetition. It represents the distance at which you want the repeating detail component to repeat. It doesn't have to be the actual width of the detail component.

Detail Rotation   This option allows you to rotate the detail component in the repeating detail.

Insulation

The best way to think of the Insulation tool is as a premade repeating detail. You'll find this tool on the Detail panel of the Annotate tab.

Selecting this tool allows you to draw a line of batt insulation, much like a repeating detail. You can modify the width of the inserted insulation from the Options Bar (Figure 11.4). The insulation is inserted using the centerline of the line of batt, and you can shorten, lengthen, or modify the width either before or after inserting it into your view.

F I G U R E   1 1 . 4   Modifying the Insulation width in the Options Bar

Detail Groups

Detail groups are similar to blocks in AutoCAD and are a quick alternative to creating detail component families. Like modeled groups, these are a collection of graphics though contain detail lines, detail components, or any collection of 2D elements. While you will probably want to use a detail component to create something like blocking, if you plan to have the same blocking and flashing conditions in multiple locations, you can then group the flashing and blocking together and quickly replicate these pieces in other details. Like blocks in AutoCAD, manipulating one of the detail groups changes all of them consistently throughout the model.

There are two ways to make a detail group. Probably the most common is to create the detail elements you'd like to group and then select all of them. When you do, the Modify context tab appears:

1. Click the Create Group button under the Create panel to make the group.

Create

2. When you're prompted for a group name, name the group something clear like **Window Head Flashing** or **Office Layout 1** rather than accepting the default name Revit Architecture wants to give it (Group 1, Group 2, and so on).

The other way to create a detail group is as follows:

1. Go to the Annotate tab's Detail Group flyout and click the Create Group button. You are prompted for the type of group (Model or Detail) as well as a group name.

Model Model groups contain model elements (elements that are visible in more than one view). Choose Model if you want elements to be visible in more than one view or if they are 3D geometry.

Detail Detail groups contain 2D detail elements and are visible only within the view you're in (you can copy or use them in other views). Choose Detail if you're creating a group containing detail lines or other annotations and 2D elements.

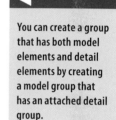

You can create a group that has both model elements and detail elements by creating a model group that has an attached detail group.

When you select the elements, you're taken into Edit Group mode. A yellow transparency is overlaid on top of the view, and elements in the view appear gray.

2. To add elements to the group, click Add and then choose your selected items (Figure 11.5).

You can also remove unwanted elements.

3. When you've finished, click the green Finish check mark, and your group will be complete.

FIGURE 11.5 The Edit Group panel

You can place any group you've already made using the Place Detail Group button on the Annotate tab's Detail Group flyout. Groups insert like families, and you can choose the group you'd like to insert from the Type Selector on the Properties palette.

Linework

View

Although not part of the Annotate tab, the Linework tool is an important feature in creating good lineweights for your details. Revit Architecture does a lot to help manage your views and lineweights automatically, but it doesn't cover all the requirements all the time. Sometimes the default Revit Architecture lines are heavier or thinner than you desire for your details. This is where the Linework tool comes in handy; it allows you to modify existing lines in a view-specific context.

To use the Linework tool, follow these steps:

1. Go to the Modify tab's View panel and click the Linework button, or use the keyboard shortcut **LW**.

   You will see the familiar Line Style Type Selector panel on the right of the tab.

2. Select a line style from the list.

3. Simply choose the style you want a particular line to look like; then select that line in the view.

The lines you pick can be almost anything: cut lines of model elements, families, components, and so on. Selecting the line or boundary of an element changes the line style from whatever it was to whatever you have chosen from the Type Selector. Figure 11.6 shows a before and after of the sill detail with the linework touched up.

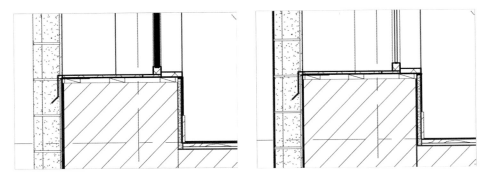

FIGURE 11.6 Before and after the Linework tool

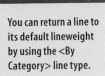

You can return a line to its default lineweight by using the <By Category> line type.

You can also choose to visually remove lines using this tool. Doing so leaves the line in the view or as a part of the 3D element but makes it effectively invisible for the sake of the view. Do this by selecting the <Invisible Lines> line type. This is a good alternative to covering unwanted linework with a masking region.

Exercise 11.1: Enhance a Detail with Regions

Enhancing your model with 2D linework and components is an efficient way to add more information to specific views without modeling everything. It is not necessary to model flashing, blocking, or other elements shown only in large-scale format detail drawings. Using detail lines, regions, and detail components, you can enhance your views to show additional design intent.

From the book's web page (www.sybex.com/go/revit2015essentials), download the c11-ex11.1start.rvt file and open the view Exterior Detl, Typ, which you'll find in the Sections (Building Section) node of the Project Browser. In the following exercise, you will create a detail and enhance the detail using filled and masking regions to accurately represent built conditions within a typical window detail:

1. Use the Callout tool on the View tab to create a new detail of the second-floor window sill: Create a new callout, and name it **Exterior Window Sill, Typ**. The starting view looks like Figure 11.7.

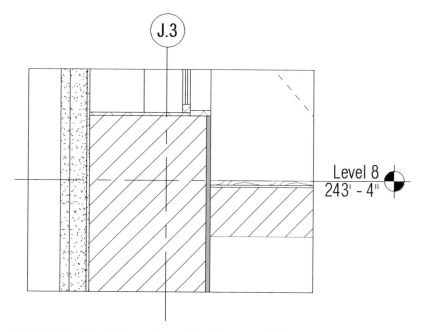

FIGURE 11.7 The window sill detail before embellishment

2. Click the Filled Region button under the Region flyout on the Annotate tab. Choose <Invisible lines> from the Line Style

Certification
Objective

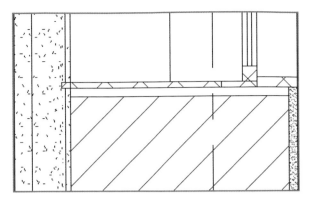

FIGURE 11.11   The completed sketch

Upon completion, your detail should resemble the c11-ex11.1end.rvt file, available in the download for this chapter. Save this detail; you'll return to it again in the next exercise.

Exercise 11.2: Add Detail Components and Detail Lines

The next step is to add some detail components for blocking and trim. From the Chapter 11 downloadable files, open the c11-ex11.2start.rvt file, or continue with your opened file if you've completed the previous exercise. Choose Application ➤ New ➤ Family, and choose Detail Item.rft. When you're creating detail components, as with any other family, you'll start with two reference planes crossing in the center of the family. This crossing point is the default insertion point of the family.

The first family, Blocking, is straightforward. You'll use Masking Region instead of the Lines tool so you have a clean, white box that you can use to layer over and mask other elements you might not want to see.

1. Select the Masking Region tool on the Create tab, and draw a box with the lower-left corner at the origin. The box should be 1″ (25 mm) high and 3″ (75 mm) wide.

2. Click the green check mark to complete the region.

3. On the Create tab, click the Line tool, and draw a line diagonally across the box to denote blocking. The family should look like Figure 11.12.

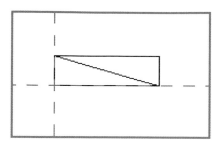

FIGURE 11.12 Creating a blocking detail component

4. Choose Application ➤ Save As ➤ Family, and name the family **06 Blocking**. Place it in a folder with the model.

5. Click the Load Into Project button at the far right on the ribbon to add the family to the model.

   If you have more than one project open, make sure you choose either your continued exercise file or the example file for this exercise, c11-ex11.2start.rvt.

6. To add the blocking detail component to your view, return to the Exterior Window Sill, Typ. detail, and click the Detail Component button from the Component flyout button on the Annotate tab.

7. Insert pieces of blocking at the left, right, and center of the sill (Figure 11.13).

The component you insert will become the default component; you can see the name 06 Blocking in the Type Selector.

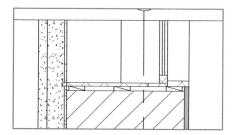

FIGURE 11.13 Inserting and placing the blocking

8. Create a new detail item using steps 1–3 for another detail component representing the baseboard (do not create a diagonal line to denote blocking), and use the dimensions 1″ (25 mm) wide by 6″ (150 mm) high.

8. The Type Properties dialog box looks like Figure 11.17. Click OK when you've finished.

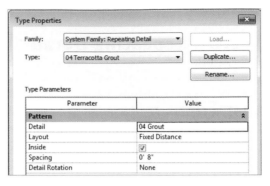

FIGURE 11.17 The repeating detail's type properties

9. With the Repeating Detail command still active, draw a line all the way up the left edge of the exterior wall, starting at the base of the view, placing the new joint over the terracotta exterior.

10. Place one of the joints directly below the window sill, by using the Nudge tool to shift the detail into the right location. This appears on top of the flashing you drew earlier, so you'll want to move the flashing to the front.

11. Select the flashing detail line, and choose Bring To Front from the Arrange panel. The completed detail looks like Figure 11.18.

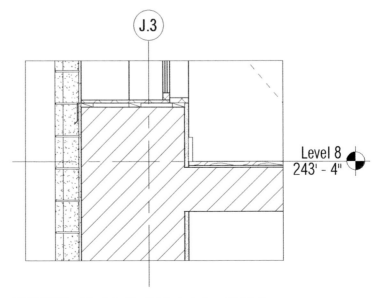

FIGURE 11.18 The finished window sill detail

Although this detail needs annotations before you can think about placing it onto a sheet, you can begin to see how you have used the 3D geometry of the model and were able to quickly add embellishment to it in order to create a working project detail. Compare your finished detail with the c11-ex11.3end .rvt file, available in the download from the book's web page. You'll return to this detail again for the next exercise.

Annotating Your Details

Certification
Objective

Notes are a critical part of communicating design and construction intent to owners and builders. No drawing set is complete without descriptions of materials and notes about the design. Now that you've created a detail, you need to add the final touches of annotations to communicate size, location, and materiality. The tools you will use for annotations are found on the same Annotate tab that you used to create details. These are the Dimension, Text, and Tag panels shown in Figure 11.19.

FIGURE 11.19 The Revit Architecture annotation tools

Dimensions

The Dimension panel is the first panel located on the Annotate tab. Revit Architecture provides you with a variety of options for dimensioning the distance between two objects, including Aligned, Linear, Angular, Radial, Diameter, and Arc Length dimensioning tools. The dimension tool you will use the most often is Aligned, located on the left side of the Dimension panel shown in Figure 11.19. It can also be found on the Quick Access toolbar . Using the Aligned dimension tool is quite simple. Click once on the first reference object to start the dimension string, and click again on the second reference object to finish the dimension.

Tags

Tags are 2D view-specific elements that attach to modeled or detail elements to report information based on that element's type or instance properties. Any modeled or detail element can be tagged; however, they are most commonly used to identify your basic building blocks—doors, windows, wall types, and

The Tag All tool is a quick way to tag everything in a view of a certain category. For example, you can tag all the windows shown in a floor plan with a single click.

◄

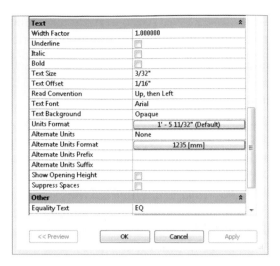

FIGURE 11.23 Dimension type properties

8. Scroll to the bottom to find the Opaque value next to the Text Background option. This controls that white box behind the dimension. Set it to Transparent, and click OK. The dimension now has a transparent background.

9. Add a dimension locating the window sill relative to the floor, as shown in Figure 11.24.

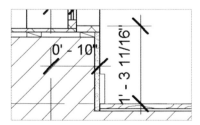

FIGURE 11.24 Dimensioning the window sill

10. To change the dimension string from the awkward length shown to a more reasonable value, you need to change the location of one of the two objects you've dimensioned. The floor probably isn't going to move, but you can reposition the window slightly. Select the window.

The dimension string turns blue, and the numbers become very small (Figure 11.25).

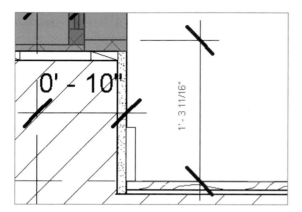

FIGURE 11.25 To change the dimension string value, change the location of the objects dimensioned by selecting the window.

11. Select the blue text, and type 1′ 4″ (400 mm) in the text box (Figure 11.26). Press Enter. The window pushes up just a bit and resets the dimension string.

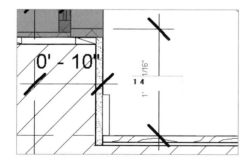

FIGURE 11.26 Entering a value into a dimension string

With all the dimensions on the detail, it should look like Figure 11.27. Compare your finished detail with the c11-ex11.4end.rvt file, available in the download from the book's web page. You'll return to this detail again for the next exercise.

4. Highlight the tag, and in the Options Bar deselect the Leader check box that is shown checked (Figure 11.30). Doing so lets you drag the tag down—leader free—and place it in the crop region.

FIGURE 11.30 Removing the leader from the Window tag

Material tags let you tag materials consistently throughout the model. If you tag something like Concrete once in the model, the material will remember the tag you used and show that same tag every time you tag it in any other view.

5. Choose the Material Tag button from the Tag panel on the Annotate tab. With the tag selected, mouse over the vertical panel shown in Figure 11.31. The material there has been prepopulated with 5/8″ GYPSUM BOARD as a tag through the material (from the Manage tab). Select the material, and place the tag.

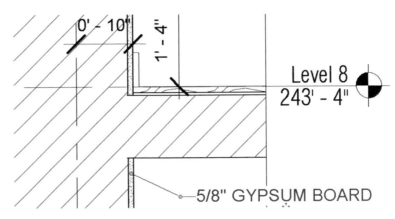

FIGURE 11.31 Using the Material tag

For materials that aren't already specified, Revit Architecture will display a question mark. Click the Material tag, and enter the text describing that material. Changes made to this material will be broadcast throughout the model.

6. Notice that by default the tag has no arrowhead. Select the tag, and choose Edit Type from the Properties palette. Here in the tag's Type Properties dialog, you can assign an arrowhead. Choose 30 Degree Arrow for the Leader Arrowhead property, and click OK (Figure 11.32).

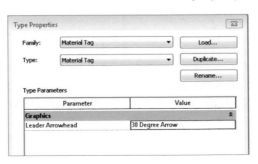

FIGURE 11.32 Adding an arrowhead to the tag

7. Choose the Text command on the Annotate tab. Doing so opens the Modify Text tab. The tools on the Format panel control the leaders, leader location, justification, and font formats, respectively.

8. For now, leave the selections at the defaults, choose a location on the screen, and click the left mouse button. Doing so begins a text box. Type **1/2″ SHIMS** (Figure 11.33). Click the mouse to finish the text and hit Esc to clear the active command.

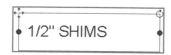

FIGURE 11.33 Adding text to the detail

9. Select the text you just created. To add a leader, click the Add Leader button at the upper left of the Format panel ⁺A.

10. Move the text and leader into position with the other notes. In this way, you can complete the annotations on the detail (Figure 11.34) and begin the next one.

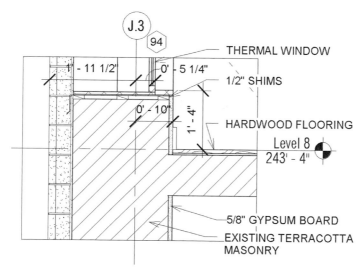

FIGURE 11.34 Finishing the detail

Compare your finished detail with the c11-ex11.5end.rvt file, available in the download from the book's web page.

Creating Legends

Certification Objective

Legends are unique views in Revit Architecture because you can place them on more than one sheet, which is not typical for most view types. These can be great tools for things such as general notes, key plans, or any other view type you want to be consistent across several sheets. It's important to note that anything you place inside a legend view—doors, walls, windows, and so on—will not appear or be counted in any schedules. Legend elements live outside of any quantities present in the model.

The Legend tool is located on the View tab. You can create two types of legends from this menu: a *legend*, which is a graphic display, or a *keynote legend*, which is a text-based schedule. Both legend types can be placed on multiple sheets, but for the following exercise, you'll focus on the legend.

The simplest type of legend would include notes such as general plan or demolition comments that would appear in each of your floor plans. More complex legends include modeled elements, such as walls.

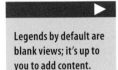

Legends by default are blank views; it's up to you to add content.

You can add modeled elements to the legend view by expanding the Families tree in the Project Browser and navigating to the chosen family. Once a modeled element is added to a legend, you'll notice three sections on the Modify | Legend Components settings in the Options Bar. This menu is consistent for any of the family types you insert.

Family   This drop-down menu allows you to select different family types and operates just like the Type Selector does for other elements in the model.

View   The View option lets you change the type of view from Plan to Section.

Host Length   This option changes the overall length (or, in the case of sections, height) of the element selected.

As part of the sample workflow, you may want to present some of the wall types as part of your presentation package to demonstrate the Sound Transmission Class (STC) of the walls and the overall wall assembly. Because these wall types will appear on all the sheets where you use them in the plan, you'll make them using a legend.

Exercise 11.6: Create a Legend

From the Chapter 11 downloadable files, open the `c11-ex11.6start.rvt` file, or continue with your opened file if you've completed the previous exercise.

1. Choose the Legend button on the View tab's Legends flyout. Creating a new legend is much like creating a new drafting view.

   A New Legend View dialog box opens (Figure 11.35), where you can name the legend and set the scale.

2. Name this legend **WALL LEGEND**, and choose 1″ = 1′-0″ (1:10) for the scale. Click OK to create the legend.

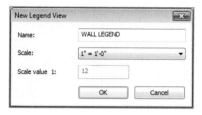

FIGURE 11.35 Creating a legend

3. To add wall types or any other family to the legend view, expand the Families tree in the Project Browser and navigate to the Walls family. Expand this node, and then expand the Basic Wall node.

4. Select the Interior – Gyp 4 7/8″ wall type, and drag it into the legend view.

5. Change the view's detail level in the view's Properties palette from Coarse to Medium or Fine so you can see the detail in the wall.

   Remember, you can turn off the thicker lines in the view by clicking the Thin Lines button 📧 in the Quick Access Toolbar (QAT).

6. Highlight the inserted wall, and look at the Modify | Legend Components settings in the Options Bar (Figure 11.36).

FIGURE 11.36 Select a legend component to access its properties in the Options Bar.

7. Change View to Section, and change Host Length to 1′-6″ (500 mm).

   The wall now looks like a sectional element. By adding some simple text and detail components, you can embellish the wall type to better explain the elements you're viewing (Figure 11.37).

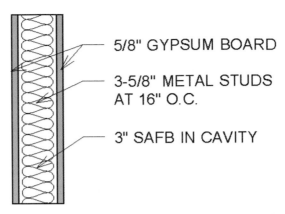

FIGURE 11.37 Add other annotations and detail components to embellish the wall-type section.

8. Continue the exercise by adding the Exterior – Brick wall type to the legend along with some additional text notes.

Compare your finished legend with the `c11-ex11.6end.rvt` file, available in the files you downloaded from the book's web page.

Now You Know

In this chapter you have learned to create a detail and enhance the detail with 2D elements— filled regions, masking regions, detail lines, and components—to more accurately represent built conditions. You have also learned to annotate the detail using dimensions, tags, and text to convey more information. In addition, you have created a legend to show typical wall assemblies in your project.

The process of embellishing a model to reflect the design intent and detailing gets easier with practice. Remember that you won't have all the geometry you need in the 3D model to show the level of detail you'll need for full documentation. By embellishing the callouts and sections with additional information, you can quickly add the detailed information you need to show.

CHAPTER 12

Drawing Sets

While the building industry moves towards a building information model as a contract deliverable, we still need to produce 2D documents for construction and permitting purposes. Using the Autodesk® Revit® Architecture software, you can create these sets of drawings with more accuracy than in the past.

In this chapter, you'll learn to:

▶ **Create a window schedule**

▶ **Create a room schedule**

▶ **Create a sheet list**

▶ **Customize schedules**

▶ **Arrange plan views on a sheet**

▶ **Activate and deactivate views**

▶ **Adjust crop regions**

▶ **Add schedules to a sheet**

▶ **Specify a sheet set for printing**

▶ **Adjust print settings**

▶ **Print documents**

Schedules

Schedules are lists of model elements and their properties. They can be used to itemize building objects such as walls, doors, and windows; calculate quantities, areas, and volumes; and list elements, such as the number of sheets, keynotes, and so on. Schedules are a valuable, spreadsheet-based way to view information about the building objects in a model. Once created,

► Width

► Height

► Count

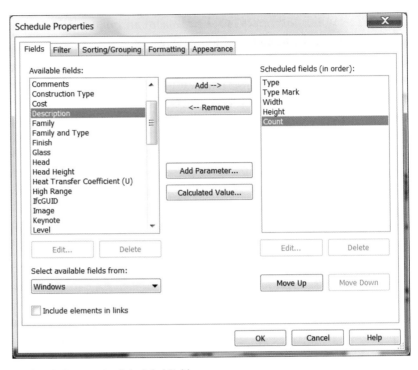

FIGURE 12.2 Scheduled Fields

5. Click the Filter tab at the top of the dialog. Choose to filter by Type Mark, and then click does not equal from the drop-down list to the right. Finally, choose A from the last column. This allows you to remove certain window types from your New Window Schedule when desired (Figure 12.3).

FIGURE 12.3 Schedule filter

6. Click the Sorting/Grouping tab. From the Sort by drop-down, choose Type. Uncheck the Itemize Every Instance option, which is located at the bottom left of the dialog.

7. Click the Formatting tab, and select Count from the Fields list on the left. Change the Alignment setting to Right. Then choose the Type Mark field from the list on the left, and change Alignment to Center so all the letters will align nicely.

8. Click the Appearance tab, check the Outline field, and choose Wide Lines from the drop-down. You will see this graphic formatting of the schedule only when it is placed on a sheet (Figure 12.4). We'll get to that later in this chapter.

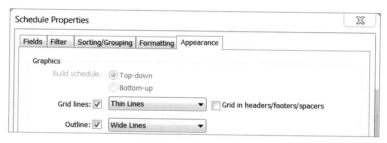

FIGURE 12.4 Schedule appearance

9. Click OK to commit all of these Schedule Properties changes. Revit opens your new schedule. In the schedule view, you can alter the column heading names by clicking inside the spreadsheet cells. Let's change the first column to **OPENING** and the second column to **TYPE**. Your schedule view should appear as shown in Figure 12.5.

		<New Window Schedule>		
A	**B**	**C**	**D**	**E**
OPENING	TYPE	Width	Height	Count
18" x 54"	D	1' - 6"	4' - 8"	1
18" x 64.75"	H	1' - 6"	5' - 4 3/4"	1
28" x 63.5"	C	2' - 4"	5' - 3 1/2"	1
29" X 48"	F	2' - 5"	4' - 0"	1
29" x 60"	E	2' - 5"	5' - 0"	6
29" x 64 3/4	G	2' - 5"	5' - 4 3/4"	1
34" x 82"	B	2' - 10"	6' - 10"	2
36" X 12"	J	3' - 0"	1' - 0"	2

FIGURE 12.5 The New Window Schedule

10. Now look in the Properties palette of the schedule view, and find the Phasing header. Under it you will find the Phase Filter parameter. Set it to Show New and click Apply, or move your mouse into the schedule. Notice that the list of windows is much shorter now (Figure 12.6). Remember, in step 3 you set the phase of the schedule to New Construction; however, this phase setting does not customize the display of the elements in the schedule view. The Phase Filter view property is required to exclude model elements that were demolished in a previous phase.

<New Window Schedule>				
A	**B**	**C**	**D**	**E**
OPENING	TYPE	Width	Height	Count
18" x 54"	D	1' - 6"	4' - 8"	1
28" x 63.5"	C	2' - 4"	5' - 3 1/2"	1
34" x 82"	B	2' - 10"	6' - 10"	1
36" X 12"	J	3' - 0"	1' - 0"	2

FIGURE 12.6 New Window Schedule

11. This concludes Exercise 12.1. You can compare your results with the sample file `c12-ex-12.1end.rvt` in the files you downloaded from the Sybex website for this book.

MULTI-CATEGORY SCHEDULES

You can create schedules that include more than one category. Perhaps you want to schedule all the windows and doors together. The way to accomplish this is to choose the <Multi-Category> option from the top of the Category list in the New Schedule dialog. One limitation of the Multi-Category schedule is that you cannot schedule host elements such as walls, floors, and ceilings when using this type of schedule.

Exercise 12.2: Create a Room Schedule

Creating other schedule types is fairly simple if you follow the guidelines we just discussed as you step through the tabs in the Schedule Properties dialog box. You have one schedule under your belt, so let's try another—this time you'll create a room schedule.

USING RIBBON COMMANDS IN A SCHEDULE VIEW

Schedules have their own special tab on the ribbon when you are in a schedule view.

A key feature of this Modify Schedules tab is the Highlight In Model button on the far right of the ribbon. This button allows you to select any element in the schedule row and locate that element in the model. Let's say you want to locate a particular window from your window schedule. Click the row in the schedule, and click the Highlight In Model button; you will be taken to a different view with that window instance highlighted.

To begin this exercise, open the file c12-ex-12.2start.rvt from the files you downloaded for this chapter.

1. Let's try a different method for starting a new schedule. In the Project Browser, right-click the Schedules/Quantities node, and then select New Schedule/Quantities (Figure 12.7).

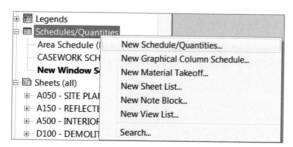

FIGURE 12.7 Start a new schedule from the Project Browser.

2. Choose Rooms from the Category list in the New Schedule dialog box, verify that the phase is New Construction, and click OK.

3. In the Fields tab of the Schedule Properties dialog, add the following fields from the Available fields column to the Scheduled fields column (in order):

   ▶ Number

   ▶ Name

   ▶ Floor Finish

   ▶ North Wall

   ▶ East Wall

   ▶ South Wall

   ▶ West Wall

   ▶ Area

   ▶ Comments

4. Click the Filter tab and choose Filter by Name, does not equal, Room. This will filter out rooms that haven't been updated with a specific name representing their function (Figure 12.8).

FIGURE 12.8   Filter out unnamed rooms.

5. On the Sorting/Grouping tab, sort by number, and then make sure the Itemize every instance option is checked in the lower-left corner.

6. On the Formatting tab, select the Area field, and set the alignment to Right. Multi-select the North, East, South, and West Walls by holding down Ctrl when you click them; then set the alignment to Center. Click OK to get the schedule you see in Figure 12.9.

	<Room Schedule>							
A	**B**	**C**	**D**	**E**	**F**	**G**	**H**	**I**
Number	Name	Floor Finish	North Wall	East Wall	South Wall	West Wall	Area	Comments
100	LIVING ROO	WOOD					307 SF	a.
101	DINING RO	WOOD					99 SF	a.
102	OFFICE	WOOD					71 SF	a.
103	1/2 BATH	WOOD					25 SF	a.
104	KITCHEN						134 SF	
200	BEDROOM	WOOD					161 SF	a.
201	BATH 1						39 SF	
202	BEDROOM	WOOD					121 SF	a.
203	BATH 2						41 SF	
205	HALL	WOOD					95 SF	a.

FIGURE 12.9 Room schedule

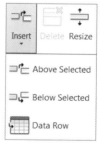

7. Now add a header to the four wall finish columns so you can visually group them. Click in the <Room Schedule> field (the brackets denote that this text is reporting the View Name parameter value). Find the Rows panel on the ribbon. Click Insert ➤ Below Selected. Notice that you now have a row of headers corresponding to the columns below (Figure 12.10).

	<Room Schedule>							
A	**B**	**C**	**D**	**E**	**F**	**G**	**H**	**I**
Name	Number	Floor Finish	North Wall	East Wall	South Wall	West Wall	Area	Comments

FIGURE 12.10 New row inserted

8. Hold down the Shift key, and click the four cells that are directly above the D, E, F, and G columns. With the four columns selected, click the Merge Unmerge button in the Titles & Headers panel of the ribbon. This gives you one large cell. Now type **Wall Finishes** into this cell. Select the cells above A, B, and C using the Shift key to select them all, and then click Merge Unmerge; name this header **Room Information**. Merge the cells above columns H and I as well, and name this header **Area**.

9. You can add data about the room elements while in the schedule view (Figure 12.11). This is quite a bit easier than selecting the room elements individually in a floor plan and inputting data about the wall finishes. Click into the cell for the Living Room, North Wall, and type in **Beige Paint**. When you click into another cell of the same column, you can choose the previous text from the drop-down. You can change all of the cells to Beige Paint if you like.

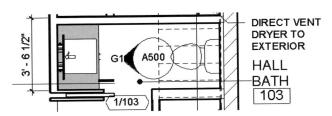

<Room Schedule>								
Room Information			Wall Finishes				Area	
A	B	C	D	E	F	G	H	I
100	LIVING ROO	WOOD	Beige Paint				307 SF	a.
101	DINING RO	WOOD	Beige Paint				99 SF	a.
102	OFFICE	WOOD	Beige Paint				71 SF	a.
103	HALL BATH	WOOD	Beige Paint				25 SF	a.
104	KITCHEN		Beige Paint				134 SF	
200	BEDROOM	WOOD	Beige Paint				161 SF	a.
201	BATH 1		Beige Paint				39 SF	
202	BEDROOM	WOOD	Beige Paint				121 SF	a.
203	BATH 2		Beige Paint				41 SF	
205	HALL	WOOD	Beige Paint				95 SF	a.

FIGURE 12.11 The finished room schedule

10. You can edit existing information, like the names of the rooms. Change the name of 1/2 BATH to HALL BATH by clicking into its cell, deleting the old text, and typing the new text. Now open Floor Plans, Level 1, and zoom into the bathroom; you'll notice that the room name has updated in the plan (Figure 12.12)!

FIGURE 12.12 The updated room name in plan view

Creating a View List schedule can help you manage your project's views efficiently, especially when using the filtering built into schedules.

11. This ends Exercise 12.2. You can compare your results with the sample file c12-ex-12.2end.rvt in the files you downloaded from the Sybex website.

Exercise 12.3: Create a Sheet List

The last kind of schedule we'll discuss is a sheet list, which creates a customized list of drawing sheets in your project. This can be especially useful on larger projects where the sheet list can get long.

To begin this exercise, open the file c12-ex-12.3start.rvt from the download for this chapter.

1. Select the Sheet List tool from the Schedules button on the View tab. The Sheet List Properties dialog box appears, starting with the Fields tab.

2. Move the Sheet Number and Sheet Name fields from the list on the left to the column on the right.

3. On the Filter tab, choose to filter by Sheet Number. From the next drop-down, choose begins with.

4. In the third field, enter the letter **A**. (Be sure to use an uppercase *A*, because Revit filters are case sensitive.) The filter should look like Figure 12.13.

FIGURE 12.13 Create a filter for specific sheets.

5. On the Sorting/Grouping tab, choose to sort by Sheet Number, and make sure the Itemize every instance is checked.

6. When you've finished, click OK to close the dialog box. You should have a schedule with only sheet numbers that begin with the letter *A*. You can drag the right-most edge of column B to make room for the full sheet name if necessary (Figure 12.14).

<Sheet List>	
A	**B**
Sheet Number	Sheet Name
A050	SITE PLAN
A100	FLOOR PLANS
A150	REFLECTED CEILING PLANS
A500	INTERIOR ELEVATIONS

FIGURE 12.14 The filtered Sheet List

7. With the sheet list view still active, click the Insert button in the Rows panel of the ribbon; then choose Data Row. You should see a row appear with a sheet name defined as Unnamed.

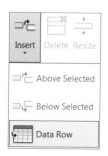

8. Change the name to **FLOOR PLANS** and the number to **A100**. You have created a placeholder sheet. These are useful when creating an outline sheet set and filling in sheet parameters, before you create an actual sheet with a titleblock in your project.

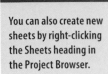

You can also create new sheets by right-clicking the Sheets heading in the Project Browser.

9. Click the View tab of the ribbon; then find the Sheet Composition panel and click the Sheet button.

10. In the New Sheet dialog box, choose the Sheets CD C1 22 × 34 : Sheets - CD - C1 titleblock and select A100 - FLOOR PLANS from the list of placeholder sheets below (Figure 12.15).

11. Click OK to create the new sheet. You'll notice in the new sheet that the sheet number and sheet name have been automatically set using the information you added to the sheet list when the sheet was a placeholder.

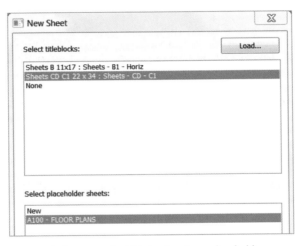

FIGURE 12.15   Add sheets using a placeholder.

12. This ends Exercise 12.3. You can compare your results with the sample file `c12-ex-12.3end.rvt` in the files you downloaded from the Sybex website.

Placing Views on Sheets

You can use the placeholder sheet feature to create a cartoon set, where the index of drawings may be planned in advance. As the design progresses and sheets are created, the design team can pick from the list of placeholder sheets.

Throughout this book, you have created several different kinds of views, from plans to elevations to perspectives. Eventually, you will need to lay out those views on sheets so they can be printed or converted to PDF and sent to clients or team members for review. Let's walk through laying out these views on sheets and see how each view can be further manipulated once it's placed on a sheet.

Exercise 12.4: Arrange Plan Views on a Sheet

To begin this exercise, open the file c12-ex-12.4start.rvt from the files you downloaded earlier.

A series of views has already been created in the exercise file. Let's use the sheet you just made and place some views on it using a simple drag-and-drop procedure:

1. Open the example file, and you should be on sheet A100. If not, expand the Sheets node of the Project Browser, and then double-click sheet A100 - FLOOR PLANS.

2. Under the Views heading in the Project Browser, find Floor Plans, and expand the tree to locate the plan view Basement. Click the Basement view and drag the view out of the Project Browser and drop it onto sheet A100. Release the left mouse button, and the outline of the view displays. Click anywhere to complete the placement of the view.

3. You can always adjust the location of the view on the sheet (Figure 12.16). The arrow keys on the keyboard are good for nudging the view.

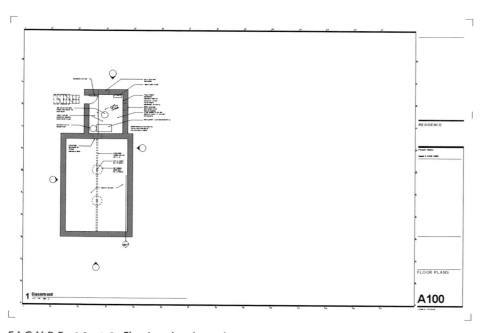

FIGURE 12.16 The view placed on a sheet

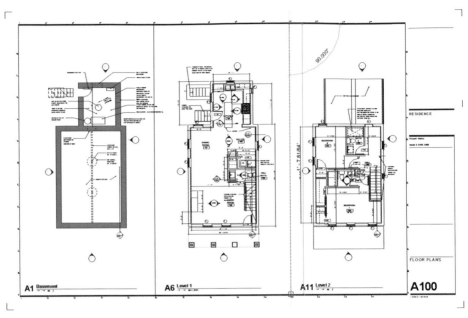

FIGURE 12.20 Adding lines to the sheet

The Revit workflow of activating a view to make changes in the context of a sheet is much like working in a model-space viewport while in paper space using the Autodesk® AutoCAD® software.

10. With these dividing lines in place, some of the text annotations in the Basement view are crossing the dividing line onto the Level 1 floor plan you added to the sheet; see Figure 12.21.

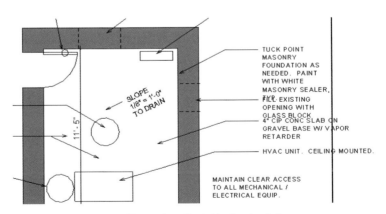

FIGURE 12.21 Text to be adjusted in the sheet view

11. Right-click the Basement view, and choose Activate View from the context menu (Figure 12.22). You can also double-click your mouse on the view to activate it.

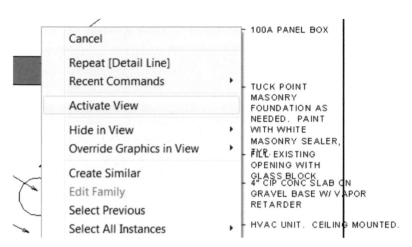

FIGURE 12.22 Activate the Basement view.

12. With the view activated, notice that the other views on the sheet have become grayed out. Select the text box you want to adjust, and drag the right grip toward the left so the text wraps and no longer crosses the line (Figure 12.23).

You must deactivate the view before moving on to other steps. The Deactivate View command is available in the context menu.

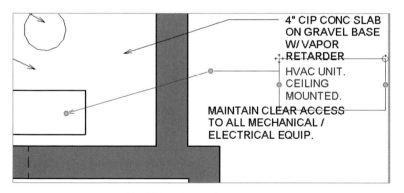

FIGURE 12.23 Modifying the text box

13. To complete your edits, you need to deactivate the view. Right-click on the Basement view, and choose Deactivate View from the context menu.

14. This ends Exercise 12.4. You can compare your results with the sample file c12-ex-12.4end.rvt available in the download from the Sybex website.

Exercise 12.5: Adjust Crop Regions

One very important aspect of composing views on sheets is to adjust the size of the view port so that only the most pertinent information is shown in the view. This helps to make an accurate set of drawings for the builder and estimator.

Open the file c12-ex-12.5start.rvt you downloaded previously to get started.

1. The file should open to sheet K100 – KITCHEN LAYOUT.

2. Zoom into view 1 called Kitchen. This is an enlarged plan of the kitchen layout, and it doesn't fit into the sheet boundary.

Activate View

Viewport

3. Select the view, and from the ribbon's contextual panel at the far right, click the Activate View button.

4. Once the view is activated, select the crop region bordering the view. Notice the blue, circular grips that appear at the midpoint of each edge (Figure 12.24). These are used for dragging interactively.

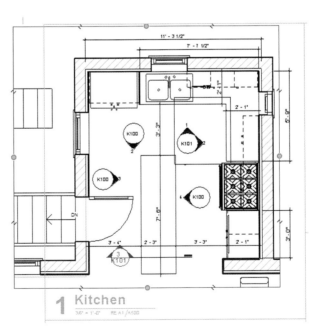

FIGURE 12.24 Crop region grips

5. Drag the left grip so that the view fits inside the sheet boundary. Revit allows you to customize the shape of your view beyond a simple rectangle.

6. Select the view again, and then click the Edit Crop button from the contextual panel on the ribbon. Now you are in a sketch mode where the crop region boundary lines are pink and the rest of the model is visible but grayed out. This is very similar to editing a floor sketch boundary. Note the Draw panel in the ribbon.

7. Select the Line tool. Draw two lines and then trim them to form an L-shaped crop that excludes the kitchen door.

8. When your screen is similar to Figure 12.25, click the green check mark to finish editing the sketch.

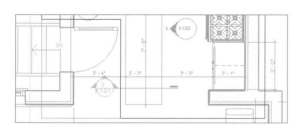

FIGURE 12.25 An L-shaped crop region

9. Now turn off the visibility of the crop region by clicking the Hide Crop Region button. The View Control Bar at the bottom of the canvas has many useful buttons; the one we care about has a crop symbol and a light bulb.

10. Click this, and notice that the crop region is no longer visible, but it is still masking unwanted areas.

11. Finally, right-click and choose Deactivate View. This is a simple example, but adjusting crop regions in the context of other views on sheets is an essential Revit skill you'll use often. The finished plan is shown in Figure 12.26.

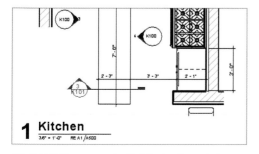

FIGURE 12.26 Finished enlarged plan

This ends Exercise 12.5. You can compare your results with the sample file `c12-ex-12.5end.rvt` in the files you downloaded previously.

Exercise 12.6: Add Schedules to Sheets

With your sheet of floor plans and kitchen details composed, you can finish the sheet set by adding the schedules you created earlier. Adding a schedule to a sheet is like adding any other view—you drag and drop it from the Project Browser onto the sheet.

To begin, open the file `c12-ex-12.6start.rvt` from the download.

1. The file should open to the sheet named G000 – COVER SHEET.

2. Find the Schedules/Quantities node of the Project Browser. Grab the New Window Schedule from the Project Browser; then drag and drop it onto an open area on the sheet.

3. Repeat this process for the Room Schedule and the Sheet List. Notice that the dotted blue alignment line appears and helps you line up the left edges so the final layout looks like Figure 12.17. You can redefine the column width of your schedules on the sheet.

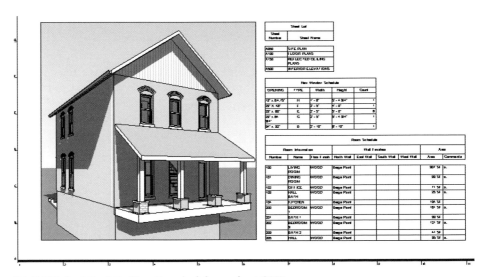

FIGURE 12.27 Place the schedules on sheet G000.

4. Start by selecting the Sheet List schedule. The schedule turns blue, and inverted triangle grips appear at the top of each column.

5. Grab one, and drag it left or right to change the column sizing.

This ends Exercise 12.6. You can compare your results with the sample file `c12-ex-12.6end.rvt` in the downloaded files.

FIXING SCHEDULES THAT RUN OFF THE SHEET

You can *split* larger schedules to make them easier to read on the sheet. When you select a schedule, you'll notice a blue cut symbol. This cut symbol lets you break the schedule into parts while on the same sheet. This can be especially handy if you have a long schedule, such as a room or door schedule that has too many rows to fit on your sheet vertically. Selecting this break symbol splits the schedule in half (and you can split it into half again and again). If you choose to separate your schedule in this fashion, it retains all the necessary information and continues to automatically fill dynamically as a single schedule would. You can also change the overall height of the schedule once it is broken by grabbing the grips at the bottom of the schedule and dragging them up or down.

Printing Documents

You will eventually need to print or create PDFs of your documentation sheets from Revit Architecture. You'll find that printing from Revit Architecture is straightforward because the process resembles that used in other Windows-based applications.

Exercise 12.7: Explore the Print Dialog Box

Open the downloaded file `c12-ex-12.7start.rvt` to begin this exercise.

1. To begin printing, you do not need to be in any particular view or sheet. Click the Application menu and then select the Print button to open the Print dialog (or use the keyboard shortcut Ctrl+P). There are several groups of settings for us to discuss.

2. Choose the printer you want to use from the Name drop-down menu at the top of the Print dialog. This can be a physical printer or a virtual one (such as Adobe PDF).

FIGURE 12.30 Print Setup dialog

14. Now you're back to the Print dialog. If you click OK, Revit will move forward with the printing process, sending the selected drawings to the printer listed at the top of the dialog. If you click Close, then the changes made in the dialog are saved, and the dialog closes without printing.

15. In the case that your print set includes some views with shading or other graphics effects like shadows, Revit will show you a warning similar to Figure 12.31. This means that Revit will use raster processing instead of vector processing for these views. See the following sidebar for some additional information about the differences between vector and raster processing.

16. This ends Exercise 12.7. You can compare your results with the sample file c12-ex-12.7end.rvt in the files you downloaded earlier.

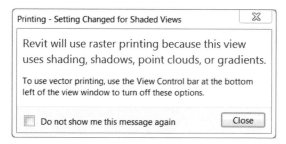

FIGURE 12.31 Raster printing is required for some effects.

USING VECTOR OR RASTER PRINT PROCESSING

Views in Revit Architecture can be displayed in several visual styles: Wireframe, Hidden Line, Shaded, Consistent Colors, and Realistic.

The Hidden Line visual style is generally used for construction documents and can utilize vector processing, which is faster and creates sharper edges.

The Shaded, Consistent Colors, and Realistic visual styles are generally used for presentation views, and they require raster processing to handle color gradients, shadows, and other graphic effects. Raster is slower and creates pixelated edges, but it also creates output that is the same as the screen display. If you choose raster, you can specify low-, medium-, high-, or presentation-quality output in the Print Setup dialog.

NOW YOU KNOW

This chapter illustrated how to move your Revit project from modeling to documentation using schedules, sheets, views, and printing. You learned how to quantify windows, rooms, and sheet elements in the model by using a schedule. Then you learned to place views, edit views, adjust crop regions, and compose sheets. Finally, you learned how to adjust the print settings to get your model information printed out.

CHAPTER 13

Workflow and Site Modeling

Understanding the Autodesk® Revit® Architecture software and how to use it is not a difficult challenge. The real challenge is determining how using Revit Architecture and building information modeling (BIM) will change your organization's culture and your project's workflow, especially if you're coming from a CAD-based environment. Revit Architecture can be more than just a different way to draw a line. In this chapter, we'll focus on what those changes are and provide some tools to help you manage the transition.

In this chapter, you'll learn to:

▶ **Staff a BIM project**

▶ **Model a site**

▶ **Create a building pad**

▶ **Purge unused families and groups**

▶ **Manage links and images**

▶ **Reduce number of views**

▶ **Maintain project warnings**

Understanding a BIM Workflow

Regardless of the workflow you have established, moving to Revit Architecture is going to be a change. You'll need tools to help transition from your current workflow to one using Revit Architecture. To begin, we'll cover some of the core differences between a CAD-based system and a BIM-based one.

Moving to BIM is a shift in how designers and contractors look at the design and documentation process throughout the entire life cycle of the project, from concept to occupancy. In a traditional CAD-based workflow, represented in Figure 13.1, each view is drawn separately with no inherent relationship between drawings. In this type of production environment, the team creates plans, sections, elevations, schedules, and perspectives and must coordinate any changes between files manually.

CAD PROJECT

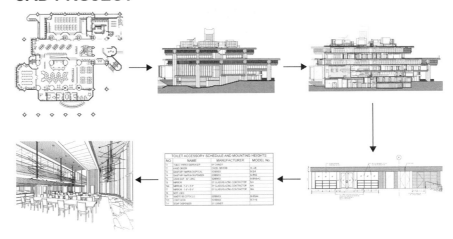

FIGURE 13.1 A CAD-based workflow

In a BIM-based workflow, the team creates a 3D, parametric model and uses this model to automatically generate the drawings necessary for documentation. Plans, sections, elevations, schedules, and perspectives are all by-products of creating an embellished BIM model, as shown in Figure 13.2. This enhanced documentation methodology not only allows for a highly coordinated drawing set but also provides the basic model geometry necessary for analysis, such as daylighting studies, energy, material takeoffs, and so on.

Using Revit Architecture becomes more than a change in software; it becomes a change in workflow and methodology. As various design specializations interact and create the building model (Figure 13.3), you can see how structure, mechanical, energy, daylight, and other factors inform design direction. You can also draw relationships between some of these elements that might not have been as obvious in a more traditional approach. Although some of these specialties (such as structure and mechanical) are historically separate systems, by integrating them into a single design model, you can see how they interact in relation to other systems within a building.

BIM

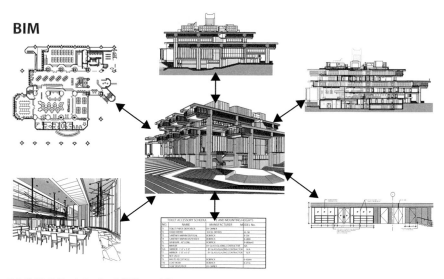

FIGURE 13.2   A BIM workflow

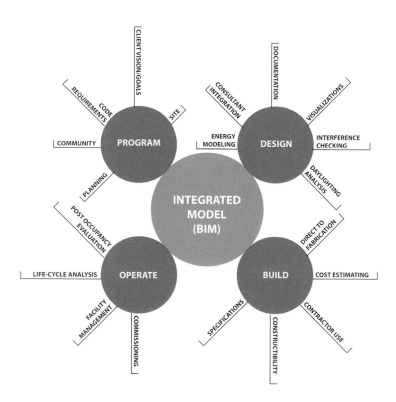

FIGURE 13.3   The integrated design model

Analysis such as daylighting can inform your building orientation and structure. Depending on your glazing, it can also affect your mechanical requirements (as solar gain). You can see some of these effects through a computational fluid dynamics (CFD) model (used to calculate airflow). Geographic information system (GIS) data will give you your relative location globally and allow you to see how much sunlight you will be receiving or what the local temperature swings will be during the course of a day. As you can see, all of these variables can easily affect building design.

Staffing a BIM Project

A common misconception of project management when teams are first moving from CAD to BIM is that staffing the project will be the same in both workflows.

As you rethink the process of design and documentation, one of the semantic changes you will need to address is staffing. When the workflow changes from CAD to BIM, staffing allocations, time to complete tasks, and percentage of work by phase are all affected as a by-product of the change of method.

In a CAD-based project, the level of effort during each of the phases is fairly well known. The industry has been using some metrics over the past several years that should be fairly familiar. There is modest effort and staffing in the conceptual design and schematic design phases, and this effort builds until it crescendos during construction documentation. At this phase, a CAD project can greatly increase the number of staff in an effort to expedite the completion of the drawing set. This staff increase can be effective because the CAD drawings are typically separate files, and moving lines in one drawing won't dynamically change another.

In a BIM-based framework, there is still a gradual increase of staffing and effort through conceptual design and into the schematic phase, but the effort during schematic design is greater using BIM than in CAD. During schematic design and design development, the project team is still performing all the same tasks that occur in any design process: testing design concepts, visualizations, or design iteration. The increase in effort during the early design phases lets the team use the parametric nature of the model to significantly reduce the effort later during construction documents, allowing for a decrease in the overall effort over the project cycle.

Project Roles Using Revit Architecture

With such a significant change in the effort behind a BIM-based project flow, it's also important to understand how this can change the various roles and responsibilities for the project team. The changes in traditional roles can become a barrier to many projects successfully adopting BIM. Project managers need to be able to predict staffing and time to complete tasks throughout the project phases and have relied on the past precedent of staff and project types to do this. Because a BIM-based project can significantly alter the project workflow, many of the historic timetables for task completion are no longer valid. However, a BIM-based project can be broken down into a few primary roles that will allow you some level of predictability through the various project phases. Although the specific effort and staffing will vary between offices (and even projects), some general roles will need to be accounted for on every project.

There are three primary roles on every BIM project.

Architect Deals with design issues, code compliances, clear widths, wall types, and so on

Modeler Creates content in 2D or in 3D

Drafter Deals with annotations, sheet layout, view creation, and detail creation

These roles represent efforts and general tasks that you need to take into account on any Revit Architecture project. We'll now cover each of these in a bit more detail and discuss how these roles interact with the project cycle.

On a large project, these roles could also represent individual people, whereas in a smaller project they might be all the same person, or one person might carry multiple roles.

Architect

The role of the architect is to deal with the architectural issues revolving around the project. As the model is being created, you will naturally have to solve issues such as constructability and wall types, set corridor widths, deal with department areas, and deal with other issues involving either codes or the overall architectural design. This role will be the one applying standards to the project (as in wall types, keynotes, and so on) and organizing the document set. This role will need to be present on the project from the beginning to ensure consistency of the virtual building creation and isn't necessarily limited to only one person.

This role also might or might not be a "designer." Although it is possible to do early design in Revit Architecture, many project teams prefer to utilize other tools such as Trimble SketchUp or even pencil and trace paper. The job of the architect is steering the creation of the building in Revit Architecture. Tasks for this role include the following:

▶ Leading the creation of massing (if used) and major architectural elements and then building from within the model

▶ Designing around code requirements and other building logistics

▶ Ensuring constructability and detailing aspects of the design

Modeler

The role of the modeler is to create all the 2D and especially the 3D content needed in the project. This content includes all the parametric families for elements such as windows, doors, casework, wall types, stairs, railings, and furnishings. Typically, this role is the responsibility of less experienced staff who might not be able to fulfill the role of architect. These less experienced positions tend to have longer periods of undisturbed time, making them better suited to deal with some of the longer, more involved tasks in modeling content. Finally, they also tend to have some 3D experience coming out of school. They might not have worked with Revit Architecture directly but possibly with Autodesk® 3ds Max® or Trimble SketchUp and are thereby familiar with working in a 3D environment. Tasks for this role include the following:

- ▶ Exchanging any generic elements used during early design stages for more specific building elements
- ▶ Creating and adding new family components and modifying existing components in the project
- ▶ Regularly reviewing and eliminating project warnings

Drafter

The role of the drafter is to create sheets and views and embellish those views with annotations or other 2D content. This role will be doing the bulk of the work needed to document the project. In earlier stages of the project, this role is typically assumed by either the architect or the modeler, but as documentation gets moving into high gear, it can quickly become the role of multiple people on a larger project. Tasks for this role include the following:

- ▶ Keynoting
- ▶ Dimensioning
- ▶ Setting up sheets and views
- ▶ Creating schedules

For a staffing-planning purpose, we are discussing the ideal times to bring in some of these various roles into the project. At the inception of a project design, a modeling role will be of the best use. This person can help create the building form, add conceptual content, and get the massing for the building established. If you're using the conceptual modeling tools, the modeler can even do some early sustainable design calculations.

Once the design begins to settle down, you'll need an architect role to step into the project. Since the design is more resolved, it's a good time to begin applying specific materials and wall types and validating spatial requirements and the owner's program. The process of moving from the general "what" something is and "where" it is to the more specific "how" something is going to be assembled isn't new. It's the same process that was used to create both traditional and modern buildings (Figure 13.4).

FIGURE 13.4 Traditional and modern designs

During schematic design, you'll need to include the role of the drafter to begin laying out sheets and creating views. These sheets and views don't have to be for a construction document set yet, but you'll have to establish views for any schematic design submittals. If these views are set up properly, they can be reused later for design development and construction-document submittals as the model continues to gain a greater level of detail.

Adding Team Members to Fight Fires

In many projects, there comes a time when the schedule gets tight and project management wants to add more staff to a project to meet a specific deadline. In a 2D CAD environment, new team members would be added to help meet a deadline and would have the burden of trying to learn the architecture of the building, the thoughts behind its design, and how its various systems interact. In a Revit Architecture project, they have that same obligation, but they have the additional task of learning how the *model* goes together. The model will have constraints set against various elements (such as locking a corridor width) as well as various digital construction issues (such as how floors and walls might be tied together, what the various family names are, or workset organization). This ramping-up period consumes additional time.

Regardless of planning, deadlines escape the best of architects and project managers. It's a good idea to know when and how you can staff to make sure you meet deadlines. Keep in mind that any team members new to the project have to learn about *both* the design and the model they have been thrown into; follow these suggestions so new staff can help production and don't accidentally break anything along the way:

Create content, content, content.   You will find that you are making model families or detail components until the end of the project. This process will help get the newbie engaged in a specific part of the project and also isolate them until they learn more about how the model has gone together.

Put them into a drafting role.   Even if this isn't their ultimate role on the project, having staff new to the design help create views and lay out sheets will get them familiar with the architecture while still allowing the team to progress on the document set.

Start them to work on detailing.   Every project can always use someone who knows how to put a building together. If you have someone new to the project and possibly even new to Revit Architecture, let them embellish some of the views already created and laid out on sheets. These views can be layered with 2D components, linework, and annotations.

> ▶
>
> What you'd like to avoid, if possible, is adding staff during the construction-document phase. In a BIM/Revit Architecture workflow, this can sometimes cause more problems than it solves and slow down the team rather than get work done faster.

Modeling a Site

In the previous sections of this chapter, you learned about the fundamental roles and workflow for your project team. Now let's talk about some other less frequently used tools. Another set of tools you should become familiar with are the site tools. They allow you to create a context in which your building models can be situated. For example, a toposurface will create a hatched area when you view your building in a section, and it will function as a hosting surface for site components such as trees, shrubs, parking spaces, accessories, and vehicles (Figure 13.5).

FIGURE 13.5 A toposurface can host components such as trees, entourage, and vehicles.

The site tools in Revit Architecture are intended only to be used for the creation of basic elements, including topography, property lines, and building pads. Although editing utilities are available to manipulate the site elements, these tools are not meant to be used for civil engineering like the functionality found in Autodesk® AutoCAD® Civil 3D®.

In the following sections, you'll learn about the different ways to create and modify a toposurface and how to model a building pad in a toposurface.

Toposurface

As its name suggests, a toposurface is a surface-based representation of the topography context supporting a project. It is not modeled as a solid in Revit Architecture; however, a toposurface will appear as if it were a solid in any section cut view, as in the 3D view with a section box enabled shown in Figure 13.6.

Certification
Objective

Toposurface

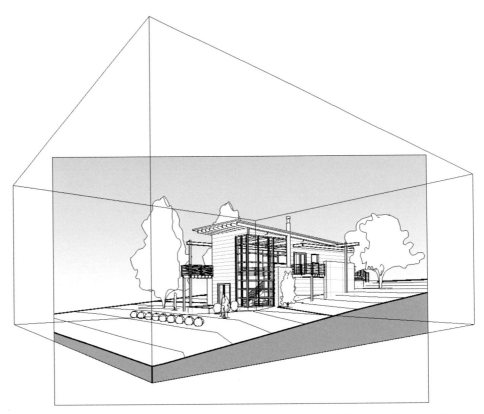

FIGURE 13.6 A toposurface appears as a solid in a 3D view only if a section box is used.

You can create a toposurface in three ways: by placing points at specific elevations, by using a linked CAD file with lines or points at varying elevations, or by using a points file generated by a civil-engineering application. You'll create a site from an imported CAD file in the first exercise.

A common workflow you may encounter when creating the topography context involves the use of CAD data generated by a civil engineer. In this case, the engineer must create a file with 3D data. Blocks, circles, and contour polylines must exist in the CAD file at the appropriate vertical elevation to be used in the process of generating a toposurface in Revit Architecture.

Building Pad

A *building pad* in Revit Architecture is a unique model element that resembles a floor. It can have a thickness and compound structure, it is associated with a level, and it can be sloped using slope arrows while you're sketching its boundary. The building pad is different from a floor because it will automatically cut through a toposurface, defining the outline for your building's garden level or basement.

Exercise 13.1: Model a Toposurface

In the following exercise, you will download a sample DWG file with contour polylines. You must link the file into your Revit Architecture project before creating the toposurface. Here are the steps:

1. Create a new Revit Architecture project using the Architectural Template.

2. Download the file c13-ex13.1Site.dwg from this book's web page, www.sybex.com/go/revit2015essentials.

3. Activate the floor plan named Site in the Project Browser.

    Certification Objective

4. Go to the Insert tab in the ribbon, and click the Link CAD button. Select the c13-ex13.1Site.dwg file, and set the following options:

    ▶ Current View Only: Unchecked

    ▶ Import Units: Auto-Detect

    ▶ Positioning: Auto – Center To Center

    ▶ Place At: Level 1

5. Click Open to close the dialog box and complete the insertion of the CAD link. Open a default 3D view to examine the results (Figure 13.7).

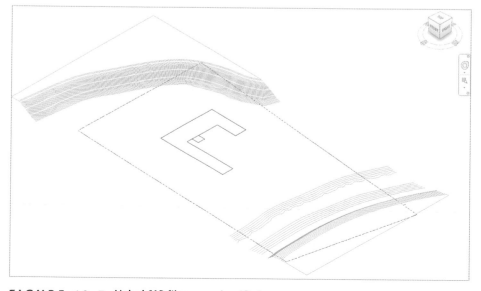

FIGURE 13.7 Linked CAD file as seen in a 3D view

6. Click the Toposurface button on the Massing & Site tab in the ribbon.

7. In the Tools panel on the Modify | Edit Surface tab, select Create From Import and then choose Select Import Instance.

8. Click the linked CAD file, and the Add Points From Selected Layers dialog box appears (Figure 13.8).

9. Click the Check None button, and then select the layers C-TOPO-MAJR and C-TOPO-MINR.

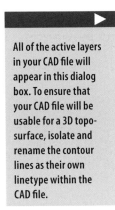

All of the active layers in your CAD file will appear in this dialog box. To ensure that your CAD file will be usable for a 3D topo-surface, isolate and rename the contour lines as their own linetype within the CAD file.

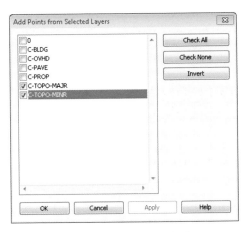

FIGURE 13.8 Select only the layers containing 3D contour information.

10. Click OK to close the dialog box. Revit Architecture may take a few seconds to generate the points based on the contour polylines in the linked file, but they will appear as black squares when they have all been placed.

11. If you want to use fewer points to define the toposurface, click the Simplify Surface button in the contextual ribbon, and enter a larger value such as 1′-0″ (300 mm), and click OK.

12. Click the Finish Surface button in the contextual ribbon to complete the toposurface. Change the visual style of the view to Consistent Colors to examine your results.

Upon completion, your toposurface should resemble c13-ex13.1end.rvt file, available for download from the book's web page.

Exercise 13.2: Create a Building Pad

The process to create a building pad is virtually identical to that of creating a floor. Let's run through a quick exercise to create a building pad in a sample project:

1. Download the file c13-ex13.2start.rvt from this book's web page and open it.

2. Activate the floor plan named Site in the Project Browser. You see an existing topographic surface and a property line. Notice that reference planes were created to demarcate the required zoning setbacks from the property line. Foundation walls have been created in these reference planes.

3. Activate the Cellar floor plan from the Project Browser.

4. Go to the Massing & Site tab in the ribbon, and click the Building Pad button.

5. In the Properties palette, change the Height Offset From Level value to 0.

6. Switch to Pick Walls mode, if not already selected, in the Draw panel of the contextual ribbon, and then click the inside edges of the four foundation walls. You can use the Tab+select method to place all four lines at once.

7. Click the Finish Edit Mode button in the contextual ribbon to complete the sketch.

8. Double-click the section head in the plan view to examine your results. Notice that the top of the building pad is at the Cellar level and the poche of the topographic surface has been removed in the space of the cellar (Figure 13.9).

You don't have to create a property line and walls before creating a building pad. You might create a building pad before any other building elements.

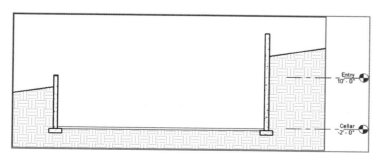

FIGURE 13.9 This section view illustrates how the building pad adjusts the extents of the topographic surface.

Upon completion, your building pad should resemble c13-ex13.2end.rvt file, available for download from the book's web page.

ADJUSTING THE SECTION POCHE FOR TOPOGRAPHIC SURFACES

If you want to customize the settings for the fill pattern and depth of the poche, click the small arrow at the lower right of the Model Site panel on the Massing & Site tab of the ribbon to open the Site Settings dialog box shown here:

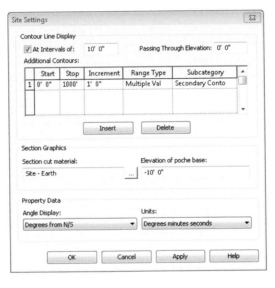

Performing Quality Control on Your Model: Keeping an Eye on File Size

You can take several measures to ensure that your model is a smooth-running and efficient machine. From time to time, ideally after major project milestones, someone on the project team should oversee the following steps to manage your model's file size and number of warnings.

Watch the size of your file. It's a good metric for general file stability. A typical Revit Architecture file size for a project in construction documents will be between 100 MB and 250 MB (250 MB is on the high side of file sizes). Beyond that, you will find that the model will be slow to open and hard to rotate in 3D views, and other views, such as building elevations and overall plans, will also be slow to open.

Should your file become large or unwieldy, you have several ways to trim the file down and get the model lean and responsive again.

Purging Unused Families and Groups

On the Manage tab is a command called Purge Unused. This command removes all the unused families and groups from your model by deleting them. Many times in a design process you will change window types or wall types or swap one set of families for another. Even if those elements are not being used in the project, they are being stored in the file, and therefore when the file is opened, they are being loaded into memory. Depending on the stage of your project, you should periodically delete these elements from the model to keep your file size down.

Don't worry—if you find you need a family you've removed, you can always reload it.

Purge Unused

Select the Manage tab, and choose Purge Unused on the Settings panel. Depending on the size of your model and how many families you have loaded, it might take Revit Architecture a few minutes to complete this command.

After Revit Architecture is done thinking, it will provide you with a list of all the families and groups in the file that are not actively in a view (Figure 13.10). At this point, you have the option to select the elements you want to delete or to keep and remove the rest.

FIGURE 13.10   The Purge Unused dialog box

We don't recommend you use this command in the early stages of design, mainly because your file size won't be that large early on and purging at this stage would eliminate any preloaded families that you might have included in your template. During schematic design and design development, you are typically going through design iteration and will likely be adding and removing content regularly. It can become a hassle to have to constantly load or reload families into the model. If your model is not suffering from performance issues or the file size isn't unruly, it's not necessary to perform a Purge Unused command.

Managing Links and Images

Another way to manage your project's file size is to remove all unused linked files and raster images from your model. If you've linked CAD files from your civil engineer or other consultants and no longer need them as a reference in your model, removing them will also unload that stored data from your model. In addition, if you've imported raster images into your project, deleting them can significantly reduce your file size. It is good practice to periodically remove these types of files from your model, especially after major deadlines, if they are not actively being used in your project.

To access these options, find the Manage Project panel on the Manage tab. Notice the Manage Links and Manage Images tools. These two commands allow you to remove any linked CAD files, Revit files, Point Cloud files, or DWF files, as well as any raster images not required for your project. Click Manage Links to remove any unwanted files, browse to the appropriate tab, select the file to delete, and click Remove. Manage Images works similarly; click Manage Images, highlight the image you want to remove, and click Delete.

Cutting Down on the Number of Views

The ability to quickly create views in a model is one of the fast and easy benefits of using Revit Architecture. This ability can also be a detriment, though, if it is not managed. Beyond the hassle of having to sort through many views to find the one you need, having too many views in Revit Architecture can also impact your performance and file size.

Obviously, a number of views are needed in the model to create the construction documentation. In addition, you will find yourself creating views to study the design, deal with model creation, or view the building or project from a new angle. These types of working views will never make it to the sheet set, and some will be used only for brief periods.

How Many Working Views Is Too Many?

How many working views is too many to have in your model? The obvious answer is that when performance begins to suffer, you need to start looking at ways to make the model lean and speed up response times. We had a project team new to Revit Architecture, and they were complaining about the file being slow to open and manipulate. When we reviewed their model, the file size was around 800 MB! We were surprised that they were able to do any work at all.

One of the first things we did to get the file size down was look at all the views that were not on sheets. More than 1,200 views were not being used. Deleting those views, paired with a Compact File save (found in the File Save Options dialog box), reduced the file size to 500 MB. Although the result was still high, you can see the impact that keeping too many views has on file size.

Dealing with Warnings

An important way to troubleshoot your model is to use the Review Warnings tool. This tool will do very little to affect your overall file size, but it will alert you to problems in the model. Warnings should regularly be addressed to ensure file stability. To open the Review Warnings dialog box, shown in Figure 13.11, click the Warnings button on the Inquiry panel of the Manage tab. The dialog box lists all warnings still active in your project file.

FIGURE 13.11   The Warnings dialog box

Certification
Objective
Errors and warnings are all essentially types of issues Revit Architecture has when it tries to resolve geometry, conflicts, or formulas that do not equate. Things that appear in this dialog box include instances of multiple elements sitting directly on top of each other, thereby creating inaccurate schedule counts; wall joints that do not properly clean themselves up; wall and room separation lines overlapping; stairs that have the wrong number of risers between floors; and so on. This dialog box shows you all the times the yellow warning box appeared in the bottom-right corner of the screen and you ignored it. Errors that go unchecked can compound to create other errors and can also lead to inaccurate reporting in schedules or even file corruption. Check the Warnings dialog box regularly as part of your periodic file maintenance, and try to keep the number of instances to a minimum.

Notice that the Warnings dialog box has an Export feature. Use this feature to export your error list to an HTML file so you can read it at your leisure outside the model environment (Figure 13.12). You can also pull this list into a Microsoft Word or Excel document so you can distribute the errors across the team to be resolved.

PhillipsPlace Error Report (12/18/2013 10:29:11 PM)

Error message	Elements
Highlighted walls are attached to, but miss, the highlighted targets.	Workset1 : Walls : Basic Wall : Interior - 4 7/8" Partition : id 230670 Workset1 : Floors : Floor : Wood Joist 8" - Attic : id 682650
Highlighted walls are attached to, but miss, the highlighted targets.	Workset1 : Walls : Basic Wall : Generic - 5" : id 260324 Workset1 : Ceilings : Compound Ceiling : TYPE B - GWB on Furring - Mark SLOPED : id 712355
Highlighted walls are attached to, but miss, the highlighted targets.	Workset1 : Ceilings : Compound Ceiling : TYPE A - 3/8" Laminated Drywall - Mark 8' - 3" : id 546901 Workset1 : Walls : Basic Wall : Generic - 6" : id 941926
Highlighted walls are attached to, but miss, the highlighted targets.	Workset1 : Floors : Floor : Wood Joist 8" - Attic : id 682650 Workset1 : Walls : Basic Wall : Interior - 4 7/8" Partition : id 722087
Highlighted elements are joined but do not intersect.	Workset1 : Walls : Basic Wall : Exterior - Existing Wood Shake : id 199956 Workset1 : Walls : Basic Wall : Interior - 5 1/2" Partition : id 212840
Highlighted elements are joined but do not intersect.	Workset1 : Walls : Basic Wall : Interior - 5 1/2" Partition : id 207075 Type : Workset1 : Walls : Chimney 5 : Chimney 5 : id 285404
Highlighted elements are joined but do not intersect.	Workset1 : Walls : Basic Wall : Generic - 15" : id 213525 Workset1 : Walls : Basic Wall : Interior - Type 4A -2 1/2" Furring Partition Foundation Wall : id 1319154
Highlighted elements are joined but do not intersect.	Workset1 : Walls : Basic Wall : Generic - 15" : id 214350 Workset1 : Walls : Basic Wall : Interior - Type 4A -2 1/2" Furring Partition Foundation Wall : id 1319064

F I G U R E   1 3 . 1 2   Exporting errors and warnings

In the example shown in Figure 13.12, using the Phillips Place model, the file has 118 errors and warnings. How many errors in a file are too many? Much of that depends on your model, your computer's capabilities, the error types, and your deliverable. For instance, if you are delivering a BIM model to your client or to the contractor, you might have a zero-error requirement. In that case, no errors are acceptable. If you are still actively in the design phase of the project, however, you will always have some errors—it is an inescapable part of the iteration process. As you refine the drawings, errors will be resolved; and as you add new content to the model that is in need of resolution, new errors will be created. If you are not worried about a model deliverable, you can get away with having fewer than 1,000 errors in the project without too much trouble. That said, the cleaner the model, the smoother it will run.

NOW YOU KNOW

In this chapter you have learned how to transition from a 2D CAD environment to a Revit Architecture BIM workflow and staff a BIM project. You have also learned to model a site and create a building pad—some of the lesser-used (but just as important) tools in Revit Architecture. In addition, you have learned to perform quality control measures on your model—purge unused families and groups, manage links and images, reduce the number of views, and maintain project warnings—to ensure that your Revit Architecture projects are quick and responsive.

Using Revit Architecture means understanding BIM as a workflow and process at all levels in your office and at all phases of your project. Being prepared for a process change as well as a software change will help you become successful as you move into BIM.

CHAPTER 14

Repeating Objects, Best Practices, and Quick Tips

This chapter provides an overview of different methods for repeating objects in the Autodesk® Revit® Architecture software. We will also discuss tips, optimizations, and best practices to help keep your project files running smoothly.

In this chapter, you'll learn to:

▶ **Use repeating objects**

▶ **Optimize performance**

▶ **Utilize best practices**

▶ **Use quick tips and shortcuts**

▶ **Locate additional resources**

Repeating Objects

Revit Architecture offers several approaches to repeat geometry throughout your project. Some are better suited for specific conditions depending on your project, so we'll provide an overview for each, along with key takeaways.

Component Families   As outlined in Chapters 5 and 6, component families are best described as anything manufactured away from the job site and used throughout your project files. Component families are the core type of repeating object you will utilize. They can be constructed to be parametric by containing multiple types of the same family; think of one door with 10 types to represent variations in standard sizes. Component families can also be used with (and are a critical aspect of) groups, links, and assemblies.

The following are the key takeaways:

▶ Component families can contain types. Instead of creating separate door families, you can create one, and you can create multiple types within the family. Each type can be configured with parameters to flex the geometry to match specific sizes or visibility requirements.

▶ Component families can be saved outside the project as stand-alone RFA files and loaded back in or into other projects. This allows for the creation of shared libraries so the entire office or multiple offices can utilize the same components.

▶ Component families can be 2D or 3D. If a component family simply needs to be quantified or scheduled but isn't visible outside plan orientation views, it could initially be created as 2D geometry. Later if the project needs changing, the family can always be modified.

 Groups   Groups are collections of project objects such as system families, component families, or detail items. Model groups are collections of 3D geometries, whereas detail groups are strictly 2D. Groups are easily created by selecting the objects you want to include in the group and choosing Create Group on the ribbon. Creating a group will generate a single element that contains a collection of objects (which also makes it easy to move everything together). A good use case for groups is a condominium or apartment project. For typical units or apartments that will appear more than once in the project, you can select the objects and create a group. This group can then be copied or inserted at multiple project locations. Edit one group type, and all instances will update to match.

The following are the key takeaways:

▶ A group instance can automatically be converted to a link at any time by selecting the group and choosing Link on the contextual ribbon panel.

▶ Groups can be saved out of a project as stand-alone project files (right-click the group type in the Project Browser and choose Save Group).

▶ Group members can be excluded from a group instance. This is extremely powerful for groups that may have one or two variations (but otherwise are identical). Instead of creating a new group type, Tab+select the group member you want to exclude from the group instance, and click the Exclude symbol that appears near the element. Should you need the member back, Tab+select the group again, and click the Restore Excluded Group Member symbol.

▶ A wall in the project can still join with a wall inside a group.

Assemblies   Assemblies are similar in many aspects to groups but with some unique tools directed toward construction workflows. Assemblies are collections of project objects similar to groups, organized in the Project Browser, along with any associated assembly views. To create an assembly, select the objects you want to include in the view, and choose Create Assembly on the ribbon.

The following are the key takeaways:

▶ Revit automatically detects whether changes to an assembly make it unique and, if so, creates a new assembly type.

▶ Assemblies have an exclusive tool called Assembly Views. These views are organized in the Project Browser (under the assembly) and create isolated views of the specific assembly type only. To create assembly views, select an assembly, and click Create Views on the ribbon.

▶ Assemblies do not allow as many object categories to be added as groups do. There are restrictions on some object categories (they cannot be added to the assembly) such as other assembled objects, annotation/detail items, groups, imports, links, model lines, masses, rooms, images, curtain systems, stacked walls, or curtain walls.

Revit Links   Revit project files can be linked into one another. This is useful not only to divide large projects or campus buildings but also to repeat geometry. For example, your project may have identical wings or buildings on campus. The Revit project can be linked in and even allows for copies of the link to be created (all instances will update if reloaded). Links also have project-wide controls under Manage Links. Here you can reload, unload, or entirely remove the link from the host project.

The following are the key takeaways:

▶ A link can be bound into the project (which will place all geometry into a new group). Simply select the link instance and choose Bind Link on the ribbon.

▶ A link can be copied, mirrored, rotated, or further modified. There can also be multiple instances of the same link.

▶ Under Visibility/Graphic Overrides, there is a Revit Links tab. Changing the display settings between By Host View and By Linked View allows the link to follow the settings of the host view or use the appearance settings of the link view.

▶ A wall in the host project cannot join with a wall in the link.

Optimize Performance

You can optimize your hardware in a number of ways to get the most out of your configuration. You should first look at the minimum hardware specifications for a computer running Revit Architecture. Autodesk has published those requirements on its website, and they are updated with each new release of the application. You can find the current specs at www.autodesk.com/revit; choose Features and then System Requirements under the Autodesk Revit Products page. Beyond the default specifications, you can do a number of things to help keep your files nimble. This section contains some additional recommendations.

Figuring Out How Much RAM Your Project Will Need

You can use a rough formula to figure out how much memory you're actually going to need for your project. The OS and other applications such as Microsoft Outlook will use some of your RAM, but you can predict how much RAM Revit Architecture will need to work effectively. The formula is as follows:

$$(\text{model size in Explorer} \times 20) + (\text{linked file sizes} \times 20)$$
$$= \text{active RAM needed for Revit}$$

Let's look at a couple of examples to demonstrate how this works. You have a project file with no linked files, and the file size on your server is 250 MB. So, $250 \times 20 = 5{,}000$ MB, or roughly 5 GB of RAM to operate.

In another example, you have a 300 MB file, a 100 MB structural model linked in, and four CAD files at 5 MB each.

$(300 \times 20) + (100 \times 20) + (20 \times 20) = 8{,}400$ MB, or roughly 8.4 GB of RAM. For this example specifying at least 10–12 GB of RAM for the workstation would be recommended.

The one area where it can be difficult to predict, since each project file varies, is when upgrading a project. Upgrading a project is usually the most memory-intensive operation in Revit. Since it is a one-time operation (for each release), you can dedicate one workstation for this task. Specify one workstation with additional memory for upgrading, if you find it necessary.

Reducing File Size

The next area to improve model performance is to reduce your file size so you're not using as much RAM. Here are some tips to do that and thereby improve your file speed:

Close your views.   Close windows you're not using to help minimize the drain on your resources. It's easy to lose track of how many views are open, even if you're concentrating on only a few views—and the more you open, the more information you will load into active RAM. If your main view is maximized, you can use the Close Hidden Windows tool to close all the windows but your active one; on the View tab, click the Close Hidden Windows button (it's also conveniently located in the Quick Access toolbar). You can also assign this command to a keyboard shortcut such as XX.

Delete or remove unused CAD files.   While working on a project you will often want to load content from another source to be used as a background. This could be a client's CAD as-built drawings or a consultant's mechanical, electrical, and plumbing (MEP) design. You might link or import these files into your drawing and forget about them during the busy course of the project. As you've seen from the earlier tips on RAM use, all these small files add up. Getting rid of them can speed up your file and is good housekeeping. If the file is linked, you can remove it using the Manage Links button from the Insert or Manage tab. Note that the Unload button does not remove it from the Revit Architecture project. If it is inserted, right-click an instance of the CAD file, and choose Select All Instances from the context menu. Clicking Delete will then remove all the instances in the view or project depending on your Select All Instances choice.

Link instead of importing CAD files.   As a general rule, always link a CAD file rather than import it. You generally have greater control using a link than using imported geometry. The link can be removed or unloaded from the project and all views with a single action. A CAD link is similar to an Xref in Autodesk® AutoCAD® software and will update if the original CAD file is modified. An imported CAD file may be spread across several different views and is more difficult to hide or remove from specific views or the entire project. It also has no association to the original CAD file and will not subsequently update if modified outside the Revit project.

Turn on volume computation only as needed.   Calculating the volumes on a large file can slow down your model speed immensely, especially when modifying bounding elements such as walls. Volume calculations are typically turned on when exporting to gbXML, but sometimes teams forget to turn them back off again. Volumes will recalculate each time you edit a room, move a wall, or change any of the building geometry. Turn off this option using the Area And Volume Computations dialog box found below the Room & Area panel on the Architecture tab (Figure 14.1).

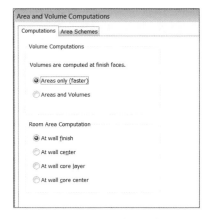

FIGURE 14.1 Choose the Areas Only setting to minimize unneeded computations.

Utilize Best Practices

Good file maintenance is critical to keeping your files running smoothly and your file sizes small. Here are some best practices and workflows identified in other areas of the book but consolidated in this section as a quick reference:

Manage the amount of information shown in views.   An overload of information in views not only will make them look cluttered but also will adversely affect project performance. Show only what you need to show in a view. Do this by minimizing the level of detail, view detail, view depth, and view content. Here are some simple tips to keep your individual views working smoothly:

Minimize the level of detail.   Set your detail level, found in the View Control Bar, relative to your drawing scale. For example, if you're working on a 1/8″ = 1′-0″ (1:100) plan, you probably don't need Detail Level set to Fine. Doing so will cause the view to have a higher level of detail than the printed sheet can show, and you'll end up with black blobs on your sheets and views that are slow to open and print.

Minimize view depth.   View depth and crop regions are great tools to enhance performance. As an example, a typical building section is shown in Figure 14.2. The default behavior causes a regeneration of all the model geometry to the full depth of that view every time you open the view. To reduce the amount of geometry that needs to be redrawn, drag the section's far clip plane (the blue dashed line when you highlight the section) in close to the cutting plane. You can also enter a more precise value in the Properties palette with the Far Clip Offset parameter.

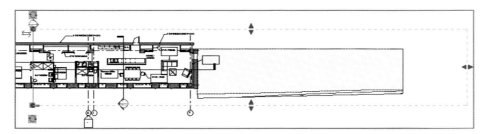

F I G U R E 1 4 . 2   Minimizing the view depth

Minimize view content.   Another best practice is to limit the amount of visible content to only what is necessary in a view. For example, in an exterior 3D view of an entire building, perhaps you can turn off categories for interior content under Visibility/ Graphic Overrides (such as electrical fixtures, plumbing fixtures, and furniture).

Model only what you need.   Although it is possible to model to a very small level of detail, don't fall into the trap of over-modeling. Be smart about what you choose to model and how much detail you show. If it's not conveying information about the project, maybe it's not needed. The amount of information you do or do not model should be based on your project size and complexity, your time frame, and your comfort level with the software.

When trying to decide how much detail to put into a model or even a family, you can use the following three very good rules of thumb to help you make the right decision for the element you're looking to create:

Scale   At what scale will this detail be seen? If it's a very small-scale detail, it might be simpler to just draw it in 2D in a drafting view.

Repetition   How many times will the element appear in the drawing set? If it will appear in only one location or only one time, it might be easier to draft it in 2D rather than try to model the element. If it will appear in several locations, modeling is probably the better solution. The more exposure an element has in the model (the more views it shows in), the more reason you have to model it. For example, doors are good to model; they show in elevations and plans all over the sheet set.

Quality   How good at modeling families in Revit Architecture are you, honestly? Don't bite off more than you can chew. If you're new to Revit Architecture, keep it simple and use 2D components. The more projects you complete, the better you'll understand the BIM workflow.

Watch out for imported geometry.   Although you have the ability to use geometry from several other file sources, use caution when doing so. Remember that everything you link into your model takes up about 20 times the file size in your system's RAM. So, linking a 60 MB NURBS-based ceiling design will equal 1.2 GB of RAM and more than likely slow down your model. Deleting unused CAD files, using linking rather than importing, and cleaning up the CAD geometry before insertion will help keep problems to a minimum.

Utilize Purge Unused.   You won't use every family and every group you create in your model. The Purge Unused tool lets you get rid of those unused elements to help keep your file sizes at a reasonable level. This too can be found on the Manage tab on the Settings panel. If a file is very large, the tool can take several minutes to run, but eventually you'll be presented with a list (Figure 14.3) of all the unused elements in your file.

▶

Using the Purge Unused tool is typically not recommended at the beginning of a project, while you are still iterating various design solutions and file sizes tend to be fairly small.

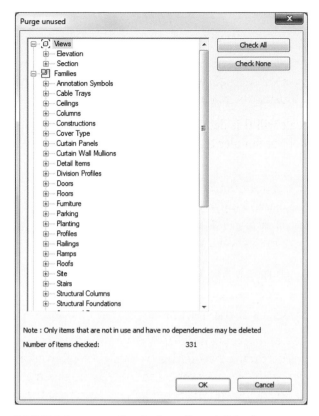

FIGURE 14.3 Use the Purge Unused dialog box to reduce file size.

Use Quick Tips and Shortcuts

In addition to all the things you can do to hone your Revit Architecture skills, you will begin to learn tips and shortcuts as your experience grows using the software. Here are some good tips to get you started:

Filter your selection.   You can filter selection behavior by customizing any combination of links, underlay elements, pinned elements, the ability to select elements by face, and the ability to drag elements on selection. For example, on a large project, you may want to disable link selection to prevent accidental selection of linked models. These options can be toggled on the fly and are available in two locations: under the Modify arrow and on the lower-right corner of the status bar (Figure 14.4).

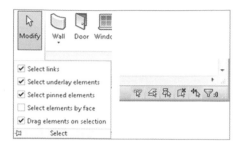

FIGURE 14.4   Selection filters

Customize your double-click behavior.   If you navigate to Application ➤ Options ➤ User Interface ➤ Double-Click Options, you can customize the action for the element types (Figure 14.5). The available actions will vary based on the element type; however, each type has a Do Nothing option. For example, if you find yourself accidentally double-clicking to edit families, you can change the default behavior.

FIGURE 14.5   Double-click settings

Make elevators visible in your plans.   Suppose you want to create a shaft that will penetrate all the floors of your building and put an elevator in it that will show in all your plans. You could do this with an elevator family and cut a series of holes in the floors by editing floor profiles, but sometimes those holes stop aligning on their own recognizance. Fortunately, you can do both things at once using the Shaft tool on the Opening panel of the Architecture tab. Here, not only can you cut a vertical hole through multiple floors as a single object, but also you can insert 2D linework (using the Symbolic Line tool when editing the shaft opening sketch) to represent the elevator in plan view (Figure 14.6). Every time the shaft is cut, you're certain to see the elevator linework.

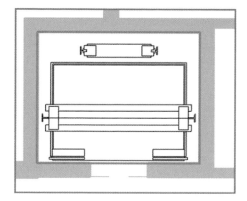

FIGURE 14.6 Adding elevators to a shaft

Orient to view. Creating perspective views of isolated design elements can be quick and easy in plan view or in section view, but let's say you want to see that same element in 3D to be able to work out the details.

1. Create a callout or section cut isolating the area in question. If you're using a section, make sure to set your view depth to something practical.

2. Open the default 3D view or any other 3D orthographic view of the project.

3. Right-click the ViewCube, select Orient To View, and select the callout or section from the context menu.

4. Your 3D view looks identical to your section or plan region, but by rotating the view, you can see that portion in 3D.

Customize your shortcuts. To edit your keyboard shortcuts, choose Application ➣ Options. Choose the User Interface tab, and then click the Customize button. You can also access this command on the View tab in the ribbon under the User Interface flyout button. The Keyboard Shortcuts dialog box (Figure 14.7) allows you to edit those shortcuts. Consider making common shortcuts the same letter. One good example for this is the Visibility/Graphic Overrides dialog box, where both VV and VG are set by default as shortcuts (VV can be used for quicker access).

FIGURE 14.7   Editing your keyboard shortcuts

Copy a 3D view between projects.   Suppose you made the perfect 3D view in your last project, and you can't figure out how to get it into your current project. Fortunately, there's a way to copy views from one project to another. Open both files in the same instance of Revit Architecture, and then do the following:

1. In your perfect view, right-click the 3D view in the Project Browser, and choose Show Camera from the context menu.

2. Press Ctrl+C to copy the selected camera.

3. In your new model, press Ctrl+V and click in the view to paste the camera. The view and all its settings are now there (alternatively you can use the Modify ➢ Paste Aligned to Current View to paste the view).

Disallow joining for walls.   By default, Revit Architecture will join walls that intersect; however, you will eventually run into a condition where you need to override this behavior. First select a wall and hover over the Drag Wall End grip. Then right-click and choose Disallow Join. This will unjoin the wall and give you additional control to drag the wall end without it automatically jumping and joining to the intersecting wall.

Join geometry on parallel walls. If you have two parallel walls and there is an opening hosted on one wall (such as a door or window), you may want to automatically cut an opening through the second wall as well. If the walls are close enough, around 1′-0″ (300 mm) of each other, you can use the Join Geometry tool between the two walls. After that, an opening will be cut in the other parallel wall and move with the original family (Figure 14.8).

FIGURE 14.8 Join geometry

Prevent room numbers from shifting on cut/paste. By default, when you cut and paste rooms in a project, the room numbers will shift to the next available numbers. There is a trick to maintain the room numbers when cutting and pasting. Select the rooms you will be cutting to the Clipboard and create a group. Once the rooms are in a group, they can be cut and pasted without changing the room numbers. Then they can be ungrouped, and the group can be deleted from the Project Browser.

Copy objects from a Revit link. Need to copy an object from a Revit link and paste it into the host project? No problem; simply hover over the object in the link you want to copy and press the Tab key until the object is highlighted. Then click to select the object and use the standard copy and paste commands. The element will be copied from the link and pasted directly into the host project, where it can be directly manipulated (Figure 14.9).

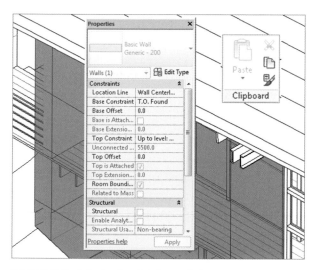

FIGURE 14.9 Copying from a link

Show annotation from a Revit link.   Some annotation objects can be displayed from a Revit link. If the link contains annotation (such as room tags, dimensions, and so on) and you want to display it in the host project, set the Visibility/Graphic Overrides properties for the Revit link to By Linked View or Custom. You can further customize which view is displayed by adjusting the Linked View name on the Basics tab.

Locate Additional Resources

A number of resources are available to help you along the way and improve your use of the software, help you solve problems, and assist you in creating new content. There is a wealth of information online to help you learn or communicate with users far and wide. So, before you spend hours trying to solve a particularly challenging problem on your own, you might check some of these tools:

Revit Architecture Help   Open the Revit Architecture Help by clicking the question-mark icon in the upper-right corner of the application. This tool will give you a basic synopsis of all the tools, buttons, and commands available in the application. It is available as a wiki at `http://wikihelp.autodesk.com/Revit`.

Subscription Support   If you have purchased Revit Architecture on subscription, Revit Subscription Support offers web-based support. Its responses are speedy, its advice is top-notch, and chances are the support staff has seen your problem before. You can access Subscription Support at `http://subscription.autodesk.com`.

AUGI   Autodesk User Group International (AUGI) is a source for tips and tricks as well as excellent user forums. The forums are free to participate in, and it's a great place where you can ask questions, find answers, and discuss project workflows. AUGI is located at `www.augi.com`. Once you're there, look for Revit Architecture.

Revit Forum   Revit Forum is an ever-growing resource with forums and collections of blog posts and has many experienced Revit users regularly participating. Registration is free, and the forums are an extremely valuable resource for common issues and workflow recommendations. Revit Forum is located at `www.revitforum.org`.

YouTube   Here's a great reason to tell your IT department you need access to YouTube. Autodesk has its own channel with great free content: `www.youtube.com/user/autodesk`. It has hundreds of short videos showing how to perform specific tasks in Revit Architecture.

AECbytes AECbytes is a website dedicated to following the trends in the AEC industry, with a strong focus on BIM, technology, and the direction of the industry. The site is put together by Lachmi Khemlani; see www.aecbytes.com.

NOW YOU KNOW

This chapter outlined the four primary methods to repeat objects in Revit Architecture (component families, groups, assemblies, and Revit Links). Every project you work on will utilize some of these object types. Next, you looked at optimizing performance, which is essential to get the most out of Revit. Best practices, quick tips, and additional resources round out the remaining portion of the chapter. This chapter should not only serve as a resource for some best practices but hopefully it provides some tips you can utilize in your projects.

APPENDIX

Autodesk Revit Architecture 2015 Certification

Autodesk certifications are industry-recognized credentials that can help you succeed in your design career, providing benefits to both you and your employer. Getting certified is a reliable validation of skills and knowledge, and it can lead to accelerated professional development, improved productivity, and enhanced credibility.

This *Autodesk Official Press* guide can be an effective component of your exam preparation. Autodesk highly recommends (and we agree!) that you schedule regular time to prepare, review the most current exam preparation roadmap available at www.autodesk.com/certification, use *Autodesk Official Press* books, take a class at an Authorized Training Center (find one nearby here: www.autodesk.com/atc), and use a variety of resources to prepare for your certification—including plenty of actual hands-on experience.

Certification Objective To help you focus your studies on the skills you'll need for these exams, the following tables show objectives that could potentially appear on an exam and in what chapter you can find information on that topic; when you go to that chapter, you'll find certification icons like the one in the margin here.

Table A.1 is for the Autodesk Revit 2015 Certified User Exam and lists the section, exam objectives, and chapter where the information is found. Table A.2 is for the Autodesk Revit 2015 Certified Professional Exam. This book will give you a foundation for the basic objectives covered on the Certified User exam, but you will need further study and hands-on practice to complete and pass the Certified Professional exam.

These Autodesk exam objectives were accurate at press time; please refer to www.autodesk.com/certification for the most current exam roadmap and objectives.

Good luck preparing for your certification!

TABLE A.1   Certified User Exam Sections and Objectives

Topic	Learning Objective	Chapter
User Interface: Definitions	Identify primary parts of the user interface (UI): tabs, application menu, InfoCenter, ribbon, Elevation tag, status bar, View Control Bar, Project Browser, context/right-click menus.	Chapter 1
User Interface: UI Navigation/ Interaction	Name the key features of the ribbon. Define how a split button works. Demonstrate the three ways the ribbon can be displayed: Full Ribbon, Min to Panel Tiles, Min to Tabs. Demonstrate how to detach a panel and move it on the screen.	Not covered
	Describe the hierarchy in the Project Browser for a new project.	Chapter 1
	Define what "context" means when right-clicking in the drawing window.	Chapter 1
	Name the tools found on the Application menu (Save, Plot, Export, Print).	Chapter 1
	Demonstrate how to add items to the Quick Access toolbar.	Not covered
	Describe why the Options Bar changes.	Chapter 1
	Describe the function of the status bar.	Chapter 1
	Describe what pressing the Escape key does.	Chapter 1
User Interface: Drawing Window	Describe what double-clicking an elevation view marker does.	Chapter 1
	Demonstrate how to turn on/off the 3D Indicator.	Not covered
	Demonstrate how to change the view scale.	Chapter 1
User Interface: Navigation Control	Describe the functionality of the ViewCube.	Chapter 1
	Describe what the ViewCube home icon does.	Chapter 1

User Interface: Zoom	Describe how to zoom using the Navigation bar.	Chapter 1
	Describe the quickest way to zoom in or out.	Chapter 1
	Describe the quickest way to pan.	Chapter 1
File Management: Definitions	Define the acronym BIM and why it is important to Revit users.	Introduction
	Define a template file.	Not covered
File Management: Project Files	Identify the file extension of a project file (.rvt).	Chapter 1
	Identify the file extension of a template file (.rte). Create a template file for later project use.	Not covered
	Identify the file extension of a Revit family file (.rfa).	Chapter 5
File Management: Open Existing Revit Project	Locate the Recent File window.	Not covered
	Demonstrate how to open a Revit file through Projects ≻ Open and through Application menu ≻ Open Documents icon.	Chapter 1
File Management: Create New Revit Project	Demonstrate how to create a new Revit project folder and file through Application menu ≻ New ≻ Project.	Chapter 1
	Change to a metric drawing.	Not covered
	Add project information to a new drawing set.	Chapter 12
	Change system settings to create a new dimension style. Change arrows to architectural tick (obliques).	Chapter 11
Views: View Control and Properties	Navigate and change views using the View Control Bar.	Chapter 2
	Understand the view range of plan views and be able to change it.	Not covered

(Continues)

TABLE A.1   *(Continued)*

Topic	Learning Objective	Chapter
	Understand the purpose of view templates.	Not covered
	Change object visibility using temporary hide, hide category, and hide element.	Chapter 9
Views: View Types	Create section views including segmented ones.	Chapter 9
	Modify, crop, and place elevation views on a sheet.	Chapter 12
	Create and navigate 3D views.	Chapter 2
	Create callouts for details.	Chapter 11
	Create and annotate a drafting view.	Chapter 11
	Use the section box to create a cutaway 3D view.	Chapter 1
Views: Cameras	Create a camera view, and modify its orientation.	Not covered
	Create and edit a walkthrough.	Not covered
Levels: Definitions	Describe a level. Describe a use of a non-story level.	Chapter 1
	Understand how levels interact with intersecting views.	Chapter 1
	Create new levels.	Chapter 1
	Understand level properties and characteristics.	Chapter 1
Walls: Architecture tab ➤ Wall	Describe how to place walls.	Chapter 2
Walls: Options Bar	List options available when placing and modifying walls: Height, Location Line, Chain, Offset, Radius.	Chapter 2
Walls: Openings	Create a floor-to-ceiling opening in a given wall.	Chapter 2
Walls: Join	Demonstrate a join on crossing wall elements.	Chapter 2

Walls: Materials	Create a new wall type, and add given materials.	Chapters 2, 9
Doors: Architecture tab ➤ Door	Describe how to place doors.	Chapter 2
Doors: Options Bar	Describe door options: Vertical/Horizontal, Tag on Placement, Leader, Leader Attachment Distance.	Chapters 2, 5
Doors: Model in Place	Edit existing doors. Use Align to position a door.	Chapters 2, 5
Windows: Architecture tab ➤ Window	Describe how to place windows.	Chapter 2
Windows: Options Bar	Describe window options: Vertical/Horizontal, Tag on Placement, Leader, Leader Attachment Distance.	Chapters 2, 5
Windows: Model in Place	Edit existing windows.	Chapter 6
Component: Options Bar	List options available when placing a component.	Chapter 5
Component: Component Host	Describe how to move a component to a different host.	Chapter 5
Component: Families	Navigate to find component families and load them.	Chapter 5
	Edit a family file and save.	Chapter 6
Columns and Grids: Definitions	Identify the uses of a grid.	Chapter 1
Columns and Grids: Architecture Tab ➤ Grid	Create an equally spaced grid pattern.	Not covered
Columns and Grids: Grid Properties	List the options available when placing and modifying grids.	Not covered
Columns and Grids: Architecture Tab ➤ Column	Place columns on a grid.	Not covered
Columns and Grids: Column Properties	List the options available when placing and modifying columns.	Not covered

(Continues)

TABLE A.1   (Continued)

Topic	Learning Objective	Chapter
Columns and Grids: Modify	List the tools you can use to modify columns and grids.	Not covered
Stairs and Railings: Stair Types and Properties	Set the stair type.	Chapter 4
	Change the stair tread depth.	Chapter 4
Stairs and Railings: Stair Placement Options	Add a stair.	Chapter 4
Stairs and Railings: Railing Types and Properties	Set the railing to rectangular.	Chapter 4
	Set the railing properties.	Chapter 4
Stairs and Railings: Railing Placement Options	Add a railing.	Chapter 4
Roofs and Floors: Roof Types and Properties	Create a roof.	Chapter 3
	Modify the roof properties.	Chapter 3
Roofs and Floors: Roof Elements	Create a fascia, a soffit, and a gutter.	Not covered
Roofs and Floors: Floor Types and Properties	Set the floor type (Sloped and Tapered). Create a floor.	Chapter 3
Sketching: Geometry	Sketch geometry and profiles using all sketching tools: Lines, Arcs, Polygons, Rectangles.	Chapter 1
Sketching: Fillet, Trim	Fillet objects.	Not covered
	Trim objects.	Chapter 1
Sketching: Snaps	Describe the benefits of using snaps.	Chapter 2
	List the shortcuts to toggle a snap on and off.	Not covered

Annotations: Text	Add model text to a floor plan.	Not covered
Annotations: Dimensions	Add a dimension to a given floor plan. Create a wall section.	Chapters 11, 12
	Add a spot slope to a roof on a given plan.	Not covered
Annotations: Tags	Add tags.	Chapter 11
	Tag untagged elements in a given floor plan.	Chapter 8
Schedules: Schedule Types	Create a door schedule.	Not covered (While there is no specific coverage of a door schedule, creating schedules is covered in Chapter 12.)
	Create a window schedule.	Chapter 12
	Create a room schedule.	Chapters 8,12
Schedules: Legends	Create a legend.	Chapter 11
Schedules: Keynotes	Add keynotes.	Chapters 12, 13
Construction Document Sets: Sheet Setup	Create a title sheet with a sheet list.	Chapter 12
Construction Document Sets: Printing	Create view/sheet sets for printing.	Chapter 12
	Print in scale. Print with percentage.	Chapter 12
Construction Document Sets: Rendering	Render.	Chapter 9
	Place generic lights.	Not covered
Set the solar angle.		Chapter 9

TABLE A.2   Certified Professional Exam Sections and Objectives

Topic	Learning Objective	Chapter
Collaboration	Copy and monitor elements in a linked file.	Not covered
	Use worksharing.	Chapter 10
	Import DWG and image files.	Chapter 13
Documentation	Create and modify filled regions.	Chapter 11
	Place detail components and repeating details.	Chapter 11
	Tag elements (doors, windows, etc.) by category.	Chapter 11
	Use dimension strings.	Chapters 1, 11
	Set the colors used in a color scheme legend.	Chapter 8
	Work with phases.	Not covered
Elements	Change elements within a curtain wall: grids, panels, mullions.	Chapter 2
	Create compound walls.	Chapter 2
	Create a stacked wall.	Chapter 2
	Differentiate system and component families.	Chapter 5
Families	Work with family Parameters.	Chapter 6
	Create a new family type.	Chapter 6
	Modify an element's type parameters.	Chapter 2
	Use Revit family templates.	Chapter 5
	Use Family creation procedures.	Chapter 6
Modeling	Assess or review warnings in Revit.	Chapter 13
	Create a building pad.	Chapter 13

	Define floors for a mass.	Chapter 7
	Create a stair with a landing.	Chapter 4
	Create elements such as floors, ceilings, or roofs.	Chapter 3
	Generate a toposurface.	Chapter 13
	Model railings.	Chapter 4
	Edit a model element's material.	Chapter 9
	Change a generic floor/ceiling/roof to a specific type.	Chapter 3
	Attach walls to a roof or ceiling.	Chapter 3
Views	Define element properties in a schedule.	Chapter 12
	Control visibility.	Chapter 1
	Use levels.	Chapter 1
	Create a duplicate view for a plan, section, elevation, drafting view, etc.	Chapter 9
	Create and manage legends.	Not covered
	Manage the view position on sheets.	Chapter 12
	Organize and sort items in a schedule.	Chapter 12

Index

Note to the Reader: Throughout this index **boldfaced** page numbers indicate primary discussions of a topic. *Italicized* page numbers indicate illustrations.